Doctor Cor

Journey
of a Medicine
Man

Richard Bartlett MD

emerge
publishing
TULSA, OKLAHOMA

Scripture quotations marked (NIV) are taken from the Holy Bible, New International Version®, NIV®. Copyright © 1973, 1978, 1984, 2011 by Biblica, Inc.™ Used by permission of Zondervan. All rights reserved worldwide. www.zondervan.com The "NIV" and "New International Version" are trademarks registered in the United States Patent and Trademark Office by Biblica, Inc.™

23 22 21   8 7 6 5 4 3 2

JOURNEY OF A MEDICINE MAN–Doctor Confirmed Miracles
Copyright ©2018 Richard Bartlett, MD

TULSA, OKLAHOMA

Published by:
Emerge Publishing, LLC
9521B Riverside Parkway, Suite 243
Tulsa, Oklahoma 74137
Phone: 888.407.4447
www.EmergePublishing.com

Library of Congress Cataloging-in-Publication Data
ISBN: 978-1-943127-82-5 Paperback
ISBN: 978-1-943127-83-2 Digital/E-book

BISAC Category:
REL045000   RELIGION / Christian Ministry / Missions
REL012110   RELIGION / Christian Life / Social Issues
SOC057000   SOCIAL SCIENCE / Disease & Health Issues

.

CONTENTS

Acknowledgements..v

Foreword..vii

Introduction..1

Chapter 1: Plan of God....................................7

Chapter 2: Man on a Mission........................25

Chapter 3: Flow of The Spirit.......................43

Chapter 4: Hope Interrupted 57

Photo Section...66

Chapter 5: Crossroads in Guatemala 89

Chapter 6: Open Doors in Kurdistan 99

Chapter 7: Preparing the Homestead...........111

Chapter 8: Demon Possession 123

Chapter 9: Revenge or Forgiveness 141

Chapter 10: On Earth as in Heaven 155

Author Bio 159

Dr. Bartlett celebrates his birthday with family and friends

Acknowledgements

Everything good in my life has come from God. I'd like to thank my wife Dawn who has been the best wife in the world, my Mom, and Dad for a great childhood, and my kids: Ben, Morgan, Grant, Zac, Daniel, Gabby, and Julia. I'd also like to thank Stefan Junaeus and Christina Hernandez for the many hours of effort it took to complete this report of what Jesus Christ did in Kurdistan. Thank you, Chuck and Helen Todd, Eva Dooley, Tim Storey and Mark Bristow for leading by example. Thank you, Barry Marks, Jose Gaona, Danny Skaggs, Dennis Skaggs, Blaine Shuffield and Wade Hudman for your friendship and prayers.

FOREWORD

There is a difference between a Good Idea and a God Idea. Good ideas may come to pass; God ideas will come to pass. Such are the journeys of Dr. Richard Paul Bartlett. In my opinion, he is the modern day Doctor Luke of the New Testament. He is a man who clearly hears from God and has decided to use his occupation and his calling to change the lives of others.

This exciting new book will take you on the missionary journeys of a man whose steps are ordered by the Lord. You will encounter the obstacles he faced, and how God gave him the inspiration and wisdom to walk through them. You will see the challenging moments, which at times looked overwhelming and somehow God provided miracles. This is a book that shows you that somebody is waiting for you on the other side of your obedience to your God Idea!

PASTOR TIM STOREY

Dr. Richard Bartlett uses a tent at the Yezidi refugee camp for an impromptu medical clinic in Northern Iraq, under the shadow of ISIS.

INTRODUCTION

"How long has it been?" I asked my ICU nurse as he checked a young Yazidi[1] woman's pulse. "Thirty minutes!" He responded after signaling to me that she still had a pulse.

I was beyond nervous. My palms were sweaty. As I kept eye contact with the three nurses who were with me, we all prayed underneath our breaths as we monitored the young woman who had not come out of a frozen catatonic state!

"How did I get here?" I asked myself. As a doctor, I knew what letting a woman die under my care, while at a Christian Church in a Muslim country, could potentially mean for myself and the team. For one, they would never let me back in the country as a missionary again. Two, in a region as dangerous as Northern Iraq,[2] lots of other bad things could happen.

Barely able to hear myself think over the loud worship and prayers of the congregation, I kept my thoughts on God. If there was ever a time I could understand what Peter felt like—when Jesus asked him to step out on the water—this was it. If I was going to avoid drowning, it was going to be because God would

---

1   https://en.wikipedia.org/wiki/Yazidis
2   https://travel.state.gov/content/passports/en/alertswarnings/iraq-travel-warning.html

1

show up. "If God could take me from a one-stoplight town in West Texas all the way to Northern Iraq," I believed, "He was going to lead me out!"

For as long as I can remember, I had wanted to be a missionary. Even in medical school, my original plan was to take my surgical skills overseas. As a doctor in a first world country, I could realistically help extend the lives of hundreds if not thousands of people over the course of a career. However, "If I could treat patients in the third world" I thought, "where even the basic medical treatments weren't available, I could extend lives by many more years."

Life has a funny way of redirecting our plans. Many of the things we plan for don't work out the way we think they will. At the same time, the things we don't end up planning for change our lives in amazing ways. That's what happened to me. After I had graduated medical school, life had other plans for me than the ones I initially had.

It wasn't until years later after I had married my wife Dawn, was a father of six children and owned my medical practice in West Texas that God revealed His divine plan for my life. Even though I wasn't a young man anymore, God wanted to send me to faraway places so that I might be a witness to His good work. Like Luke the physician, I would also be sent to retain and record. I would be an expert medical witness to the miraculous events God would perform for those who needed healing.

That's exactly what God did. He took me from West Texas,

led me across the world, all the way to Kurdistan[3] in Northern Iraq. This book is a record of those events. It's not so much my story, but a witness of many great things I have seen God do overseas. It exists to tell the world that God is alive and well. Like in the book of Acts, He is still healing, loving, and redeeming all of His creation. It's an eyewitness report of how God gave purpose to my life and thousands of others I have encountered along the way. I want everyone who reads this book to walk away convinced that you are just as qualified as anyone to be witnesses of God's incredible love!

Just like us, the disciples were flawed and complicated human beings. They were fishermen, tax collectors, and physicians. They were regular people, with normal jobs, from every part of society; ranging in age, family lineage, and socio-economic background. The same is true about those God calls today. Over the course of my journey, I've seen 90-year-old missionaries, all the way to my son who is eight years old, impact the world by telling people about Jesus and expanding God's Kingdom. If my journey has taught me anything, it's that the Great Commission is for every Christian. If God can use me to share the good news, He can share it using anyone. If you are a believer, you can do it too.

Chuck Todd,[4] the founder of World Missions Alliance[5] always says, "God doesn't call the qualified, he qualifies the called." If you feel something calling you to take a step of faith, it's prob-

3   https://en.wikipedia.org/wiki/Iraqi_Kurdistan
4   https://rfwma.org/about/chuck-todds-page/
5   https://rfwma.org/

ably God. I can tell you right now if God was faithful to me, He will be faithful to you. For when we step out in obedience by faith, that's when God honors and opens the doors for the miraculous.

God is a miracle working God. He has given us tools, **Power Tools** in Scripture and through the witness of others to do the good work of building the Kingdom. Let this book witness to you. Use it as a practical guide that can help you share the good news that God's Kingdom has arrived, wherever the Lord takes you.

India 2007

Many people reported instant relief from symptoms as a result of prayer.

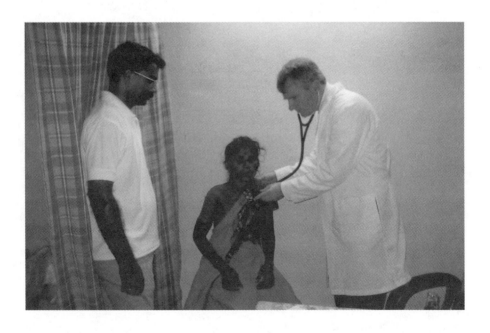

Many poor and sick walked for miles barefoot on mud roads for the rare opportunity for medical care.

CHAPTER ONE

PLAN OF GOD

*"For I know the plans I have for you," declares
the Lord, "plans to prosper you and not to harm
you, plans to give you hope and a future."*
                                        Jeremiah 29:11 NIV

On June 14, 1998, my family and I attended Sunday morning service at Cross and Crown Church in the small town of Crane,[6] Texas. Over the last few weeks, we had heard great things from our pastor about our special guest speaker, Bruce Delay. Now that he was finally here, all of us showed up, expecting something special.

After praise and worship had concluded, Bruce took the stage. He started by thanking our pastor and the church for welcoming him so generously. He was excited to share what was in his heart, to preach about Christ's love, the Holy Spirit and the power of the Lord's presence.

---

6   https://en.wikipedia.org/wiki/Crane,_Texas

About half way through the sermon, Bruce stopped abruptly in the middle of his thought and looked right at me. As he walked from the behind the pulpit to the front of it, the atmosphere shifted to a reverent silence. "Doctor Bartlett," Bruce said, "the Lord has a word for you." Completely surprised, I froze, not knowing how to respond. The congregation went silent. You could have heard a pin drop as all eyes were on Bruce and what he would say next.

"You are Luke the physician, called in My Word the Beloved Physician, for My love for you is big. Great big, says The Lord. Do not doubt My love for you. You shall be a recorder, you shall be a retainer, and you shall be a reporter of Kingdom events in your life. I will take you places, and you shall travel, says The Lord. I will take you places to witness and to see and to write and record and report and retain those things. For you are a detail man, says The Lord.

"And He says that you have much to learn in the Spirit, but you shall become a student of the Spirit. Not as much of the Word in this hour but as of the Spirit. And I shall make you a student of My Spirit. And you shall travel in the appointed time when I initiate, and I will free you up, says the Lord. I will enable you to go and to be gone, and your wife shall be able to travel with you. You will go places, and you will experience things in God that you will retain, and you shall report about. And The Lord says to take a little wine for your stomach's sake. That is, when your stomach, your spiritual stomach, is upset with worry and anxiety and all the things that come against your life; when there is an upset stomach, take a little wine.

"My Holy Spirit shall supply all that you need in that time. Pray

in the Spirit. Come to My Spirit for refreshing in those days, and take some wine for your stomach's sake, says the Lord, for it shall be medicine for you, a spiritual medicine that shall refresh you and retain you. The Lord says He is going to give you people, men and women, to bear the burden with you because you have a lot of irons in the fire. And He is going to give you trustworthy people that you can leave things with and walk away and not even have to think twice about it because He's calling you away.

"And you are not only a doctor in the natural, but you have a calling of God upon your life that must be fulfilled, it must come into focus. It is not in focus at this time, but it must come into focus in the days to come. I am calling you to an hour of knowing your future, knowing what's ahead, and beginning to prepare for it. The Beloved Physician, My Beloved Physician. The Lord says I love you because I see My love in you for people. You reflect My love for people, and that is needed in this earth. People must see My compassion and My love for people. So, go ahead, and show forth My love. Go ahead and be who you are. You don't have to be like anyone else. Just be who I have made you to be, says the Lord. Entrust Me with your future."

As I heard Bruce speak, I had no doubt I was hearing from the Lord. Years ago, when I was in high school, I knew that one day God would use me to help people overseas. In college, I took deliberate steps to prepare myself for the possibility that God would use me for international medical missions. Even though I would spend hours listening to the stories of guest doctors about their mission trips as the president of the Christian Medical Society of the Texas Tech Medical School, the door had never fully opened for me to go. As I got older, started my career, got married, and began a family, the more I had accepted that the dreams of my youth were probably not going to happen.

After hearing the Lord speak to me through Bruce, I had more questions than answers. "How will all this work?" I wondered. "Could God really be calling me to the mission field at this age?" I wasn't a young man anymore. As a doctor, husband, and father, I was managing a busy medical practice while also raising six small children. My staff and I were experiencing monumental problems at work. I, along with hundreds of other doctors, was embroiled in an ugly legal battle with a dishonest insurance company that would not pay for the care I had already provided to numerous patients. They owed my clinic over $200,000, and I was facing bankruptcy.

Aside from refusing to pay me, the insurance company used bogus and vague complaints to the Medical Board as an attempt to intimidate me to withdraw my claim. When one set of allegations were deemed "unfounded," they would file another set of complaints. For years, I felt like David when Saul was hunting him. My family and I went from one unprovoked struggle to the next. Even though we had each other, it was hard to see a break in the storm.

For the next two years, I put the prophecy Bruce had given me on a shelf and decided to focus on my immediate problems. It wasn't long before God spoke to me again. On December 9, 2000, a guest, Denny Cramer, came to the Crane church and delivered a personal prophecy to Dawn and me: "Your first name sir." "Richard" I responded.

"Hi, Richard. Richard the Lord says to you, surprise, surprise, surprise. The Lord says I'm like candid camera, My son. That when you least expect it, My son, My call is coming knocking on your door. I have recently moved in your life to give you a new set of circumstances so you can respond to the call of God. I'm doing it in you says the Lord. I will raise you up to be My man, My vessel, My spokesman. They won't be able to shut you up says the Lord. You're going to bubble up, bubble up, bubble up says the Lord. The Lord says you will be a volcanic man, you will erupt!

"Says the Lord, with wisdom and insight in the house of God, I have recently, My son, broken the restraints off your life. I've recently set you free from past constraints. And even from words spoken over you as a child. I break all the family restraints. I set you free to become not some, but all that I have called you to be. You've been afraid, My son, of what I might do with you. I did something in you first so that I might do something with you second. Ha Ha. The Lord says, I did it, I snuck up on you, and I saved you. Ha Ha. Then I snuck up on you and gave you a heart for the people of God. I did it. Yah. And you've been saying grown men don't cry. Wrong. Wrong. God says grown men do cry.

"I've given you a heart for the people of Christ. I give you a gift of tears. My son, you're a walking intercessor. You can't help it. I've given you a sensitivity for the body of Christ. I've given you the capacity to bear burdens for others. And, My son, even at times you'd watch TV, you'd languish over the suffering, the sorrows and the

misery in the world. And you've been dealing, My son, with some of your theology because some of it needs to be revised. And so I'm going to take some of that old legalism off of you. And I'm gonna fill you.

"Yes, I know. You've looked around at some of those Holy rollers and said, I will never do that. God says never say never. And the Lord says, Son, what you have wanted is the legitimate power of God to flow in you, and on you and through you. I heard that prayer. This day is a foretaste, only a foretaste, of what I have for you. My son, I've made you a theological student. Oh, you like the Hebrew, you like the Greek, you like the concordances. Mr. Three-point Sermon. Yes, Yes, Yes. You know how to lay it down, and you know how to feed it to my people. But I've heard your prayer.

"I'm going to begin to add a power dimension for your ministry that you never thought possible. I am the God that has heard your cry. So get ready to minister as never before. Get ready to preach as never before. Get ready for me to interrupt your three-point sermon, with a strong prophetic anointing. People will say, pastor, what did you do? You were right in the middle of point #2 and never did point #3. And you will become more and more and more at ease with how I'm going to interrupt your life. Because you're the one who said, "Well, I'd like to have some of that river flowing from my belly like Your Word says." I have heard that prayer, and I will flow.

"One day, you will get phone calls from other churches and they'll say, "Is this where the flow-er lives?" Ha, Ha, Yah. Are you the flow-er? And the phone will ring, and you will go here and there. And you will bring the anointing with you that I have given you. For, I will use you to start many fires. Oh, Yah. Don't be afraid of the word

Revivalist. Oh, that anointing will come upon you, and you will see the fires of revival says The Lord!

"And you, woman of God, you've been a thorn in the flesh to the kingdom of Hell. You have. I've used you as a deadly weapon. I've used you to bring confusion and dismay upon demons and devils upon the earth. Oh, they've come against you, they have. They've tried to undermine you. But you've risen up. Because I've made you a woman of faith. Ha Ha, you've risen above circumstances. Oh, the enemy came in like a flood, but I have given you a standard of praise and worship that you have raised up against it time and time again. I'm going to release praise and worship in you and through you. That gift, that talent, that level of ability that you have now…Oh ho ho ho, the Lord would say, "You ain't seen nothing yet! I'm gonna touch you. Yah, I'm going to give you more of what you got.

"Worship is all over you young lady—worship, songs and praise unto God. Yah, it's going to start in the feet, don't be afraid of the beat, don't be afraid, God says. Yah, I'm going to begin to perfect praise and worship in you. And you have and, My daughter, deep-seated fears, and even some personal objections to things you've seen, even extremes and abuses. But know this, I appreciate the thoroughness from which you approach theology. I have appreciated the careful study of My Word that you endeavored to take. I have made you a student. You might be the Greek and Hebrew guy, but you are the meditative, contemplative prayer warrior of this family. And at times, I have used you, says the Lord, even to set the pace at times.

"You've said, 'Honey, come on, we've got to get up, we've got to go. We got to go!' For I have made you fearless. I have made you fearless.

I have brought you, and I have brought you here to let you know it is time for you to step into the deeper things of God. It's time for you to pay the price. I told both of you when I brought you together in marriage: are you two married to one another? When I brought you two together in marriage, I told you both: it was for a Kingdom purpose.

"The Lord says, it will never again after today be business as usual. Never, never, never, never. The old, the old, the old is passed away. God says get ready, get ready. Wheee! Wheee! The Lord says get ready for the roller coaster ride of your lives. Yes. God says get ready, get ready, get ready, get ready! For I have appreciated your sincerity, both of you. Your commitment to My purposes, says the Lord. But get ready for a revision of theology and practices and procedures. For God says, I will pour out My Spirit in your midst, says the Lord! Amen"

Sometimes when God speaks to you, He also breathes new life into you. Two weeks before Denny Cramer prophesied over my life, I had been up late at night watching television by myself because I couldn't sleep. A few minutes into a Feed the Children[7] infomercial, I started crying while I quietly prayed for the children. For, even after two years, I still had no clear direction on how to follow the word Bruce Delany had given me.

The words of Denny Cramer shot right through my heart. As he spoke, I remembered my experience sitting in front of my television a couple of weeks before. I felt like Nathaniel in the Gospel of John when Jesus tells him, "I saw you while you were still under the fig tree before Philip called you." Jesus was

---

7   http://www.feedthechildren.org/

saying the same thing to me. Even though no one was with me as I prayed in my living room, God was there. He would order my steps.

I could feel things turning around. The huge health insurance company that had driven me towards bankruptcy was finally punished. For the first time in the history of Texas, an insurance company had been sued by the state for denying necessary care. After a federal court had found them guilty of racketeering, they settled for over $400,000,000. Even though my practice had still not been reimbursed, God proved to be my Restorer.

Just like for me, I believe that God also has a plan for your life. The Bible tells us that God knows our frame. In Jeremiah 1:5 He says, "I have known you before I formed you in your mother's womb." As your Creator, He has designed a destiny for you that He is actively calling you toward. The more you pursue that destiny, the more He will reveal to you. Psalm 37:23 says, "The steps of a good man are ordered by The Lord." When you take a step of faith, take it in confidence knowing that God will be there for the next step.

AN UNEXPECTED GOD IDEA

In 2002, I met a lab technician named Prasana. He had just opened a private medical lab in Odessa[8] and was looking for clients. Having lab tech experience myself, I asked him why I should use his lab instead of setting one up for my clinic my-

---

8   https://en.wikipedia.org/wiki/Odessa,_Texas

self? After he had shared his story, Prasana convinced me why I should partner with him.

Prasana grew up in a Christian family in the middle of the Hindu-dominated, Indian province called Andhra Pradesh.[9] Even though his family was poor, he did very well in school. His high grades gave him the opportunity to go off to college. While he was in college, he rented a one-room, dirt-floor dwelling. There were times he was so poor he could only afford one full meal a week. Regardless of his circumstances, he performed well enough to finish his education.

Once Prasana completed school, he and his wife immigrated to West Texas to work in a small town hospital. Not long after, his wife was tragically killed in a car accident. Prasana eventually took what he received from the insurance settlement and built seven churches back home in India. After Prasana had remarried, he moved to Odessa where I practiced medicine.

Year after year, Prasana invited me to visit India. Even though I was interested, every year I would turn him down. It never felt like the right time. In 2007, he asked me again. This trip he wanted to set up a free medical clinic at the churches he had helped build. After praying about it, God gave me the peace I needed to leave my practice and family. I gladly accepted his invitation.

Within a few months, I found myself in India. From the moment we landed in Hyderabad,[10] it felt like we were in an Indiana

9   https://en.wikipedia.org/wiki/Andhra_Pradesh
10   https://en.wikipedia.org/wiki/Hyderabad

Jones movie. Everything was so different from back home. The densely populated city had a run down, dingy airport. The moment I stepped off the airplane, my senses were overwhelmed by sewer vapor, body odor, and the humidity. As we made our way through the terminal, a sleepy looking security staff watched the crowd slowly make their way through customs. After retrieving our luggage, we made our way through dozens of beggars and taxi drivers along the curb, all of whom were shouting in Hindi. Finally, we reached Prasana's friend's van parked outside.

As we drove through the city in the middle of the night, there were homeless people sleeping in the creases of every building. It was what I imagined downtown Chicago looked like during the Great Depression.[11]

Desperation hung over the city just like the inescapable sewage fumes. As we approached the worn-looking railway station, the outside was lined with sleeping beggars, each with bags full of everything they owned. The sun began to dawn as we boarded the passenger car. The train looked like something out of an era long past—terribly weathered on the outside, in good repair on the inside.

Once we pulled out of the city, the air became much fresher. A man in a uniform slowly made his way down the aisle checking tickets. Another railway employee also made his way down the aisle, offering to pour each passenger a cup of scalding hot Chai (tea). The Chai[12] was excellent, and a first for me. Star-

11 https://en.wikipedia.org/wiki/Great_Depression
12 http://www.bbc.com/news/magazine-27991440

bucks had not yet opened in Odessa, Texas. As we made our way through the countryside, many shrines to Hindu gods scattered across the horizon as well as the dozens of farmers working in the fields. Almost all of them were working by hand or using oxen to pull their plows.

I also noticed there were no outhouses for the farmers. At first, seeing farm workers squatting in the distance caught me off guard. It was definitely a different culture than that of America. As the train traveled down the tracks, the passenger car rocked back and forth. I could see monkeys jumping from trees to rooftops as we passed a small village. The farmland eventually turned into mango orchards and open fields blanketed with bright green grass.

As the sun began to set, we pulled into our final destination of Vijayawada, Prasana's hometown. Vijayawada[13] had a population of just over one million people. It felt a lot like the town of Matamoros,[14] Mexico when I had visited in the 1980s.

An SUV drove us through the city. Prasana and his brothers were clearly on guard. Local businesses had barred windows and doors. Homes had high walls and gates. Prasana explained that broken glass was often embedded on the top of the walls to deter thieves. He also paid someone to guard the church's courtyard while we stayed in town.

The church had two men opening a gate to a front courtyard as we entered. The church was a concrete, two-story building

13   https://en.wikipedia.org/wiki/Vijayawada
14   https://en.wikipedia.org/wiki/Matamoros,_Tamaulipas

with a patio under a large upper balcony. As we pulled through the gate and into the courtyard, a large crowd of smiling people greeted each of us as we got out of the vehicle. As people spoke to me, I nodded a lot. I also tried to communicate with eye-contact and gestures. It was polite but ineffective at getting my thoughts across. All of us felt the genuineness of the warm welcome.

They had set up a room for me in the guest quarters at one of the churches. The first night, a swarm of giant flying insects with translucent wings blew in and filled the night sky around the church. The next morning, when I came out to the balcony, the ground and patio were covered with them. None of them were alive. After looking more closely, I noticed that all the insects' wings had fallen off. The locals were busy sweeping them up. They were keeping the bugs but discarding the wings. Later that day, they roasted them and ate them as a finger food treat. I declined.

The following night, the first monsoon rain of the season hit. The rainfall was so heavy that by morning, the roads and alleys were covered with large bullfrogs. Like the insects, the locals also gathered them for food. Prasana explained that this was a long-standing tradition. I also declined the frog meal.

Each medical clinic was set up inside one of Prasana's churches. Large banners announced the clinic outside. Crowds of locals had filled the courtyards before we arrived. As we drove down rough, muddy roads to one of the clinics, I was amazed to see people of all ages who had walked barefoot for miles in hopes of receiving medical help. Some were in bad shape; others just needed a checkup. All of them were struggling with the same kinds of medical conditions as those back in my clinic in Texas.

For the next six days, Prasana and I treated as many people as we could. With the help of a team of volunteers, who aided by taking vital signs and initial triage information, hundreds of people were able to receive treatment. Prasana even generously paid for all the medications we prescribed. Aside from providing medical care, it was important to both Prasana and me to offer prayer to each patient after their examination. Regardless of whether they were Christian or Hindu, almost everyone we treated reverently received our prayer and words of encouragement.

After the last day of clinics, Prasana wanted to take everyone who had helped to the best restaurant in town. It ended up being a Motel 6 with a surprising, beautiful buffet and salad bar.

The doorman and waiters were dressed in fancy uniforms at the standard of an exclusive casino in Monte Carlo. I decided to eat healthy. I heaped generous helpings of fresh salad of every item on my plate before having the main course. The dinner was fantastic. It felt like a celebration.

As I got back to my room, I began to feel feverish. After a few more minutes, my body began to ache. I was showing all the classic symptoms of a food-borne illness. As I got sicker, I began to pray for myself. I was scheduled to preach the next day. Ironically, I had prepared to speak on the power of prayer. The next morning, even though I felt so sick, I asked God to give me the strength to lead the service.

As I took the stage, the double front doors at the back of the church were left open. I could see the water buffalo grazing freely in the unfenced bright green field in front of the church. The men sat cross-legged on the floor on one side of the room while the women sat on the other end with a wide aisle between them. The primitive structure had minimal furnishings in the main sanctuary. The bright and colorful sarees[15] that the women wore seemed so much more vivid in such a monochromatic space. Even though the open doors offered some ventilation on such a hot day, the women fanned their faces while the men used their sleeves to wipe the sweat from their brows.

In the front of the sanctuary, Prasana and his brother played keyboard and drums while the congregation joined them in worship songs. The sweat was pouring off their faces as they played. Their clothes were completely soaked by the end.

As I listened, I was moved by how passionate and sincere the congregation's worship was. After Prasana had introduced me, I was greeted with a warm applause and plenty of smiles. Just like I had planned, I taught about prayer and the importance of praying in the Spirit. I spoke of worship, praise, thanksgiving, and intercession. After praying for the people to acquire a prayer language, the entire congregation spoke utterances in trust that the Holy Spirit was in charge of their prayers. The service ended with dozens of people lined up to be prayed for. We anointed and prayed for the sick, and many immediately felt better.

---

15   https://en.wikipedia.org/wiki/Sari

I, however, grew sicker. I was frequently in the restroom. I had never been sick like this before. The flight home was miserable. I met Barry Marks and another friend for lunch at a sandwich shop as soon as I returned. At the end of the meal, I nearly passed out as I stood up. Barry took me to a gastroenterology doctor's office. I was given three liters of IV fluids. The lab results revealed I had Hepatitis A. It took weeks to get my strength again.

DISCUSSION QUESTIONS

- Do you remember a time God spoke to you? What did He say?
- Which Bible verses discuss how God speaks to individuals?
- Does the Bible say God has a specific plan for your life? What verses?

SPIRITUAL KEYS TO SUCCESS

- Don't reject prophecy. That said, always hold it up to the scrutiny of Scripture which is the standard of all truth.
- Line up faithful friends who will pray for you day and night as the Spirit prompts.

Avoid uncooked food.

Republic of Georgia 2013

New structure called "The Museum of the Kings" overlooking the 2.5 million people of Tbilisi.

The structure is very similar to "Stonehenge" and seems to have a religious purpose but this is unknown to the populace.

CHAPTER TWO

MAN ON A MISSION

We are therefore Christ's ambassadors, as though God were making His appeal through us. We implore you on Christ's behalf: Be reconciled to God.　　　*2 Corinthians 5:20 NIV*

In the spring of 2013, a man named Chuck Todd came to the small church in Odessa, Texas that my family had been attending. Up until that Sunday, I had never heard of Chuck or his organization, World Missions Alliance before. As Chuck had shared his story and the work he was doing on the mission field, I couldn't get enough of what he had to say. I also felt a deep desire to be a part of that work. After sharing about all the places God had led him over the years, he began to talk about his latest missionary work, evangelizing the Kurds in northern Iraq.

Chuck laid out the plight of the Kurds,[16] how they had been oppressed, a nation without a home, and similar to Israel after

---

16　https://en.wikipedia.org/wiki/Kurds_in_Iraq

World War II, were finally in a position to win independence. Now, I had heard about the Kurds a few times in the past few years. Saddam Hussein[17] had hunted the Kurds as they fled to the Turkish border in an attempt to completely exterminate them. It is not an exaggeration to compare Saddam Hussein and his acts against the Kurds to Adolf Hitler's treatment of the Jews. Saddam named his campaign[18] to kill all the Kurds after a book in the Koran that translates in English to "The Spoils (of war)." Saddam Hussein's army hunted thousands of Kurds as they fled to the Turkish border attempting to escape mass genocide. In the middle of the night, Saddam's henchmen would blow up bridges and roads blocking escape routes. They then used chemical weapons to wipe out entire villages and towns,[19] not sparing any women or children.

Chuck explained that when the Syrian Civil War[20] started, the Kurds secured a region in North Syria and Northern Iraq. They hoped that an ancient dream of the Kurds[21] was coming true—a land of their own: Kurdistan. Chuck said the Kurds had established a government and had asked him to help them become a Christian nation. Even though 98% of Kurds were labeled Muslim at birth—for their parents had been labeled Muslim on Birth Certificates—most did not study or know the teaching of the Koran or practice the faith. Chuck told us that they did not exactly know what it meant to be Christian either,

17   https://en.wikipedia.org/wiki/Saddam_Hussein
18   https://en.wikipedia.org/wiki/Anfal_genocide
19   http://uk.gov.krd/genocide/pages/page.aspx?lngnr=12&pnr=37
20   https://en.wikipedia.org/wiki/Syrian_Civil_War
21   https://consortiumnews.com/2017/10/17/the-thwarted-dreams-of-kurdistan/

but they knew they didn't want to be a Muslim nation. They lived with Muslim culture all around them and did not want Islam to be the foundation of their government. The Kurds had even drafted a constitution that they were about to ratify. In that constitution, they stated that they were a Christian nation. Remember, this is Northern Iraq!

The Kurdish government leaders asked Chuck to send pastors and teachers to help them learn how to be Christians. They told Chuck that they controlled over 300 towns and villages and wanted pastors and preachers in every town and village. To aid this undertaking, they wanted Bibles in the Kurdish language. Up to this point, there had never been a Bible translated into Kurdish. Chuck had no idea how that would happen but, as an act of faith in God, he told the Kurdish leaders he would get the Bibles. Chuck was now touring American churches telling his story and raising money to translate and print 50,000 Bibles in a Kurdish dialect. Over the past few months, people had been giving generously. He only had to raise $20,000 of the $120,000 it would cost to print all the Bibles. As he finished sharing, Dawn and I felt this was a great investment in the Kingdom.

During our first encounter with Chuck, he explained that the Kurds were unique. They called themselves the descendants of the Medes,[22] cousins of Israel. In contrast to their neighbors, they had a positive relationship with Israel and the United States. In fact, in a quiet way, Israel had been aiding the Kurds for the past 30 years.

---

22   https://en.wikipedia.org/wiki/Medes

After the service, Dawn and I met Chuck. He told us about his family. We were surprised that his wife was born in Tbilisi, Georgia where our son, Zachary, was born. Most people couldn't even find Georgia, let alone the capital city of Tbilisi on a map. I did not know where Georgia was before we adopted Zachary. It was very unusual. Chuck said they had a small apartment in Tbilisi. He told us we could stay there if we ever wanted to take Zac back to visit his birthplace. The thought of going on our own seemed daunting. Zac and I don't speak Georgian or Russian. Even so, I appreciated the offer. After the service, I kept in contact with Chuck.

On June 11, 2013, another guest speaker, Eva Dooley, at Parker Heights Church prayed with our family at the end of the service. Several prophecies came forth. She told me, "You have the anointing of Obed-Edom.[23] God makes everything pertaining to your household prosper. The household has the presence of the Lord like the Ark of the Covenant. Where ever you and your family go, you have God's favor. Your house has God's glory, and every member of the family has God's glory. You would be used to open doors for others; you are like a Levite, a priest. Richard will travel around the world." Her words confirmed past prophetic words I had received. Each of them confirmed a persistent calling toward missions.

"Isn't it amazing that the calling that God had over my life did not fade with time." I kept thinking. When I heard the call years before, so many things had stood between me and the mis-

---

23   http://www1.cbn.com/devotions/who-obed-edom

sion field. Today, it was a different story. My business was doing much better, my kids were older, and as a family, we were in a much better place. All I needed now was the right opportunity.

RISKING GOOD FOR GREAT

Weeks later, I heard that World Missions Alliance was planning a mission trip to the Republic of Georgia![24] I had three months to get ready for the trip in September. At first, I was overwhelmed at the news. I had never heard of a mission trip to Georgia before. I knew that if Zac and I didn't go, there was a chance we would never get the opportunity to do it again.

After talking to Dawn about it, we decided it was a God idea to take Zac to the Republic of Georgia. Just a few years earlier, I had taken Zac's older brother, Ben, to Latvia so he could see his birth nation. Now it was Zac's turn to experience his rite of passage by visiting his birthplace. The only drawback was the timing. The trip would take place during the school year. Zachary was a senior and already enrolled in three college classes.

I also see people accepting the Lord in my practice every day. A part of me felt like it might be a bad idea to leave for those two weeks. Things were finally doing well at my practice, partly because I am always available and have God's favor. "Would things fall apart without me?" I kept asking myself. There were also family-related issues that seemed to show up all at once. There was car trouble, a few teenage emotional flare-ups, and a host of other small things. There were many logical, understandable

24   https://en.wikipedia.org/wiki/Georgia_(country)

reasons as to why Zac and I should not go on this trip. I found myself reading Scripture, looking for guidance on what I should do.

Mark 14:3-7 (NIV) says, "While he was in Bethany reclining at the table in the home of Simon, the leper, a woman came with an alabaster jar of very expensive perfume made a pure nard. She broke the jar and poured the perfume on Jesus' head. Some of those present were saying indignantly to one another, why this waste of perfume, it could have been sold for more than a year's wages and all the money given to the poor."

This seemed like a valid thought!

I continued, after "they rebuked her harshly. Jesus said, Leave her alone, why are you bothering her? She has done a beautiful thing to Me. The poor you will have with you always, and you can help them whenever you want, but you will not always have Me."

Jesus' words spoke to me on many levels. Sometimes we have to do the extravagant thing, spend more money than we normally would, to do the thing that God tells us to do. Sometimes we have to do what would seem foolish to others because we know it is God's will. It will look like the wisest decision to everyone after the fact.

Zachary is a senior, but he won't be living under my influence for that much longer. I decide that we should go on the trip. Once I made the decision, the path clears for me to travel. I find a doctor who will cover the ER. I talked to Zachary's teachers, and they gave their approval. The superintendent and the principal said to go, and that missing two weeks would not be a problem. They joined the growing chorus of people in our lives who gave us the green light, so we decided to take off.

It's Monday, September 9, 2013, when I get up early the day of the trip. My four-year-old son, Grant, is sick and congested. My son, Ben who is a college student, had developed a severe cough overnight. On the one-hour drive from Crane, Texas to the Midland airport, I pray with a friend, Danny Skaggs, by cell phone. Danny prays "that the trip will be a defining moment in Zachary's life and that Zac and my relationship will become closer on the journey." Our plane flies from Midland, Texas to Houston without trouble.

Our connecting flight from Houston to London gets delayed. We now have to wait a total of six hours before takeoff. As we waited, I notice the lady sitting next to me has a Scottish accent. I had toured Scotland before so I start talking to her about Scotland. She was waiting for the same flight and informed me that she heard the flight had been cancelled. After hurrying to the gate, I discover that the flight has indeed been cancelled! I look across the hallway, and I see that there is another flight headed to London. I decide if I can get Zach and me on that flight, we may still be able to catch the rest of our connecting flights, ensuring that our trip would not be derailed.

Once I get to the counter, the airline attendant tells me that the flight is full and that there are ten people on standby in front of me. She says it is not worth even trying to get on standby. As I walk back over to the line for my original cancelled flight, I can see dozens of other people trying to make hotel arrangements to spend the night. "This will totally mess up our connecting flights," I kept thinking. While I wait in line for assistance, I think "What do I have to lose? I am going to go over there again." I take Zach and go back over to the gate with the flight that is still scheduled to fly to London. This time, a different airline attendant is at the counter. She is very helpful and gets Zac and me on standby. Within five minutes, a miracle happens! We board the plane!

Once we arrive in London, the computer does not show us on the next connecting flight. Fortunately, the airline attendant solves that for us at the last minute. We then travel from London to Germany. In Germany, the flight attendant would not let us board. The airline did not have the right boarding passes for us, so that had to be solved first. Every step of the way, just like in life, the devil will try to do small things to deter us from doing God's will.

LAND OF STALIN

It's September 10, 2013, 3AM Tbilisi[25] time, when we arrive in the country of Georgia. "Thank God!" I thought! We wait awhile in the passport check line. As we wait, I get texts from Helen Todd,[26] co-founder of World Missions Alliance, asking where I am. She is apparently not receiving my return texts or receiving my calls either. I look at the crowds surrounding me

25   https://en.wikipedia.org/wiki/Tbilisi
26   https://rfwma.org/about/helen-todds-page/

hoping I might spot a clue as to who Helen is. For I have never met her or seen a picture of her. Of course, my name tag that was issued by World Missions Alliance is still in my checked luggage which I have not picked up at baggage claim yet.

The passport agent is very slow and seemed to act dramatic on purpose; as if that made his work more thorough. Our luggage never shows up. Chuck Todd, Helen's husband and co-founder of World Missions Alliance, calls me on my cell phone from the US. He tells me Helen is looking for me. I explain that we are having trouble with our cells connecting. We watch everyone else get their luggage, but our luggage does not appear. Finally, we find Helen in the main entrance of the airport. It is packed with people milling around, everyone pressed against each other. It takes over an hour to complete the form declaring lost luggage. Eventually, we get in the van that will take us to the hotel.

The van ride from the airport to the hotel was nothing short of interesting. Traffic was incredibly chaotic. We pass seven police cars with lights flashing while on the highway. I noticed at one point that our van and the car next to us were riding down the middle of the road lines instead of between them. With eight lanes of traffic, driving felt like a game of chicken. Traffic lanes functioned more like a suggestion than a law. I also saw a sign of George W. Bush waving. The sign indicated we were on George W. Bush highway.

I was relieved when we finally reached our destination. The Iceberg Hotel[27] was two years old. The lobby was small but nice-

---

27 http://hotel-iceberg.ge/en/

ly decorated with marble tile and a leather couch. The shower had the pressure of a car wash with plenty of hot water. The shower head was also shaped like a curling iron. Zac and I are roommates. Our first order of business is to catch some sleep!

The next morning, we met everyone on the team in the hotel lobby. As I look around, I notice how unusual our mission team is. First, there are only eight people on the team. I have seven children; Zac is the one who is gifted with a mind of business. He is money-minded. As a small child, he would sell toys and games to his younger siblings and friends at school. The only way Dawn and I knew of his business ventures was when his little brother asked us for money. Second, two members of the team, Odd Frustol, from New Jersey and Clyde Pfeiffer, from Florida, were successful businessmen. They took an early interest in being mentors to Zac. They listened to him, and Zac respectfully paid attention when they spoke. Like most teenagers, Zac had little time or interest in his elders' opinions. It seemed like a set up from the beginning. Psalm 37:23 (NIV) says, "The steps of the righteous are ordered by the Lord." Obviously, this team was handpicked by God with Zac in mind. God is in the details.

Our interpreter was a 22-year-old lady named Elza who was originally from the Ukraine.[28] Her father was an atheist who became a Christian and is now a pastor in the Republic of Georgia. Elza speaks four languages; she is a very gentle spirit. We are divided into two teams, each assigned to go to a different church in opposite directions. Half the team went west to a city named

---

28   https://en.wikipedia.org/wiki/Ukraine

Gori[29] and half went east to the town of Rustavi.[30] Zac and I "coincidentally" are sent to Gori; so four of us went to Gori from the very beginning.

RELIGIOUS TRADITIONS

On September 11, 2013, we met the pastors of two non-denominational churches in Georgia who tell us about their spiritual and political struggles. The pastors were discouraged and emotionally beaten down by the Georgian Orthodox Church.[31] The pastors told us that this Church does not teach people about God. They do not care if you have a Bible and most people do not have a Bible. Most of the Georgian public believes that because they were born in the country of Georgia, they are Christians because it is a Christian nation. In AD 337, the king of Georgia became a Christian, and he said my kingdom will be a Christian nation. After that, Georgians now have this mindset that if you are born in Georgia, you are a Christian and obviously you are Orthodox because that is the Church of Georgia. The church is a political power base. The pastors explain that the Orthodox Church teaches that anyone from another denomination is a cult. They reported the Catholic, Baptist, Methodist, Charismatic, and other Christian denominations are looked down upon and persecuted. The pastors explained that when it is found out that people are of a denomination other than Or-

---

29   https://en.wikipedia.org/wiki/Gori,_Georgia
30   https://en.wikipedia.org/wiki/Rustavi
31   https://en.wikipedia.org/wiki/Georgian_Orthodox_Church

thodox, believers can't get their work permits renewed per the pastors. They suddenly have bad credit and can't get loans, etc. How did this oppressive religious atmosphere develop?

The Georgia pastors told how this thinking was developed. The Jehovah's Witness[32] came to Georgia at the very beginning of Georgia breaking off from the USSR and according to the local pastors, proved that they were a cult. Let me explain. As opposed to every denomination that bases their beliefs on the Bible truths, Jehovah's Witness rejects the doctrine of the Trinity and the existence of hell. They teach that Jesus was not God, but God's first creation. They believe that only 144,000 people will go to heaven and they will all be Jehovah's Witness. Many Georgians think if you are not Orthodox, you might be Jehovah's Witness and in a cult. The non-denominational pastors were very discouraged by this because they were treated like cult leaders. The effect of the Jehovah's Witness organization in Georgia was to strengthen the false argument that any non-Orthodox religious group that comes to Georgia is also a cult.

Galatians 6:9-10 says, "Let us not grow weary in well doing, for at the proper time we will reap a harvest if we will not give up; therefore as we have the opportunity, let us do good to all people especially those who belong to the family of believers." Then Psalm 37:1 NIV says, "Do not fret yourselves for evildoers or be envious of them that do wrong." This is an encouraging word for the pastors.

We are told that we will each be teaching/ministering to

---

32   https://en.wikipedia.org/wiki/Jehovah%27s_Witnesses

youth the next day. Zachary and I are to meet with the youth of Gori the next day. We do some sightseeing and shopping as a group in the capital city of Tbilisi.

On September 12, I got up early. At around 7:00 a.m., our luggage arrived at the hotel while I'm still in the lobby praying and reading my Bible. Last night, I felt the Lord told me that the homeless would begin joining church groups. Many people who live by highways and byways would turn to the Lord and accept Him and enter the Kingdom.

At 8:00 a.m., we ate breakfast at the hotel. Three hours later, we rode in vans up the "Holy Mountain,"[33] as locals call it, to pray together for a mighty revival of the people of Georgia. After grabbing lunch at a restaurant on the mountain, we rode back down a tram, just in time to make it to Gori for a prayer meeting with local business owners at the small nondenominational church that evening.

During the drive, we passed three sets of refugee villages built for Georgians who lost their homes during the 2008 war[34] with Russia. Russia had invaded South Ossetia,[35] a province of Georgia. Even though the war has technically ended, the area is still occupied by Russian troops.

The countryside is noticeably beautiful. Apple orchards, vineyards, and cabbage fields are everywhere. There are also cattle and sheep in the fields. In the town of Gori, we drive past the 5th

---

33 https://www.tripadvisor.in/ShowUserReviews-g294195-d6749575-r481117462-Mount_
    Mtatsminda-Tbilisi.html
34 https://en.wikipedia.org/wiki/Russo-Georgian_War
35 https://en.wikipedia.org/wiki/South_Ossetia

Infantry Brigade Fort. While our driver is temporarily lost, we are nearly run over by an armored personnel carrier full of troops speeding down a city street.

Eventually, we reached the small church and greet the business owners who are there to meet us. After praying with them for favor, continued success, and blessings over their families, we drive back in the van from Gori to Tbilisi. There has been no evangelism in sight so far.

After what seems to be a very long drive, we finally got back in time to eat a late dinner at the hotel. Even though it's late, at 11:00 p.m. Zac decided to explore the city streets by foot. After leaving the hotel, we walked through the heart of the city. Eventually, we cross(ed) a bridge near the TV tower on top of the "Holy Mountain" before making our way back. We even decide(d) to stop at McDonald's for a snack. Once we got back, we realize(d) we've walked almost 10 miles. It's nearly 3:00 a.m.

The next day Zac and I went to a small church in Gori with two other members of the mission's team to meet with several business owners and visit their businesses. After touring a paper distribution warehouse and a beauty salon, we pray(ed) blessings over each enterprise.

On September 14, Zac and I went to the Gori church to pray with the youth group in the morning. We later went to Rustavi with the rest of the team to pray with the youth group in that church. Helen says the plan is to switch the two teams for the second half of the trip. Zac, Odd, Elise and I would be going to the Rustavi church and not Gori. I tell Helen that I don't know why but I believe God wants us to continue to go to Gori. Little did I know the connection to Gori that would soon be revealed to us.

Early the following morning, Zac and I join Odd and Elise Frustol in ministering at the Gori Sunday morning service. The young worship leaders lead some great songs in Georgian. I taught about tithing and giving through an interpreter. Odd gave the sermon. His wife Elise came up to pray for the sick. Elise prayed for each person, one at a time. They started to fall to the ground while she was praying. The local boys in the congregation started laughing, assuming they had tripped. When more people began to fall during prayer, those in the seats rushed up to the stage and pulled out an iPad and phones to capture what was happening. They had never seen this sort of spiritual manifestation before.

After the service, the pastor invited us to eat snacks with him and his wife. They had generously prepared to be gracious hosts with many treats to eat, and we visited. With Helen Todd interpreting, he told us his life story and testimony. As a young man, he joined a gang and lived a life of crime. Eventually, his actions landed him in a Russian prison for two years. It was during this tumultuous period that he received Christ as his Savior and decided to become a pastor.

DISCUSSION QUESTIONS

- Have you ever met someone who you knew was following God's amazing plan for his/her life? A history maker/ world changer?

- Have you ever felt like God was nudging you to do something that was illogical or ridiculously extravagant? Do you do it—why or why not?

- Do different regions have different spiritual strongholds? What does the Bible say about that? Why would God commission Christians to travel to foreign nations?

SPIRITUAL KEYS TO SUCCESS

- Even when the future is unclear, trust in God. For your steps are truly ordered by Him.

- If you're experiencing spiritual warfare, keeping going. The devil often tries to do small things that will deter you from doing God's will.

- Never judge a book by its cover. God can use anyone to spread the good news.

Richard and Zac miraculously find Zac's birth aunt in a remote village on the edge of a war zone between Georgia and Russia.

CHAPTER THREE

FLOW OF THE SPIRIT

"The wind blows wherever it pleases. You hear its sound, but you cannot tell where it comes from or where it is going. So it is with everyone born of the Spirit." John 3:8 NIV

While we were driving in the van, Elza, the interpreter asks, "What was Zachary's surname before he was adopted?" "I don't know," I responded.

"People from different regions in Georgia have different personality traits," she continued. "These people are really funny, they have a good sense of humor in this area. And then over in this area, they are known for walking right down the middle of the street in heavy traffic. And you know, if you told me his surname, I could tell you where he is from in Georgia."

I have never been interested in trying to contact birth givers. I did not want any confusion when raising my children. Adoptions can be emotionally complicated for kids. As his father,

I never wanted to add unnecessary pain to their lives. But for some reason, today, I felt differently about it.

I had an unusual peace about the prospect of Zac learning more about where he was born. I texted my wife and told her to text me pictures of his original adoption papers in Georgian. I received them via my cell phone. While we are driving down the road, I showed the images of the documents to Elza and Helen. They have never seen this surname before. It is Georgian, and the interpretation of the surname is Son of Christ.

"Well, that is interesting!" I thought to myself. I sent a text with that information to my wife, Dawn. She texted me back, "That makes me cry." Another document Dawn had sent me showed that Zac's birth mother was born in a little village called Bershueti, which is in the province of Gori.

Zac and I have been going to this area since the very beginning of our trip without even realizing it. It was already set up for us! No one in the van has heard of this village. We look on Google Maps, and it is not on Google Maps. It is so remote that Google does not know where this village is. That night, Elza uses a Russian computer program and is able to find the village. We look at the map on her computer and see winding, little roads leading north to the village, but it is not labeled. All of the other big roads and highways are labeled except this one. All we can tell is that the road goes north toward Russia.

Years ago, as I watched the 2008 Olympics, I remember news reporters discussing the war between Russia and Georgia. Olympic coverage had been periodically interrupted with breaking news reports of the Georgian war with Russia. The conflict was over a region called South Ossetia. Even today, the Russians still have soldiers there that are squared off in a tense cease-fire with Georgian troops along the border. The village looks like it might be in that Georgian region occupied by invading Russian soldiers.

We decide that we are going to try to find the village the next morning. That same evening, Helen Todd, our team leader, arranged for us to have dinner with some of her friends. Nada and her husband Otto were wonderful people and generous hosts. We took the subway and ate at their apartment in the middle of the capital city Tbilisi. Their apartment is located next to the only medical school in the Republic of Georgia. We heard stories of how Nada and Helen first met in Kindergarten and of the events that transpired earlier in the day. After an incredible night of fellowship, we headed back to the hotel.

On September 16, I woke up at 1:15 am anxious in the hope of finding the village of Zac's birth giver today. I took my journal with me into the hotel lobby and later to a balcony so I could write. I am alone.

While on the balcony, I noticed three things for the first time since being in Georgia, possibly a moment of clarity for good things to come. The first is that the wind is increasing; I am used to the wind since I live in West Texas. That's the reason I had noticed the lack of wind in Georgia until now. Second, lightning and storm clouds have started to gather. The skies have been clear until tonight. Third, a jet is flying through the clouds right over me. This is the only plane I've seen in the sky over the capital city since I've arrived. The storm must have diverted the jet off its main course.

That morning, breakfast is at 9:00 a.m., Helen Todd tells us her former classmate, who is now the former Georgian parallel of an FBI chief, called her and asked to meet that evening. Helen believes this is related to her presence at an organizational meeting the night before for the Billy Graham crusade that's scheduled to take place next June in Tbilisi.

FAMILY SECRETS

The morning starts with a tour of a monastery which is on the way to Gori. While we are there, Zac finds a hole in the stone floor in an empty side room. Lying on his stomach, he holds his camera in the hole and takes a picture. Studying the photograph, to his amazement, he sees a man lying on the dirt floor! In a second photo, the man has moved. Good, it is not a dead body. It appears to be a monk living a vow of poverty. None of the other tourists milling all over the property are aware of what we have discovered. It is a day of uncovering hidden secrets.

We take a short drive to a parking lot where Otto is waiting with his car to take us to find the village of Bershueti. When we get to his vehicle, he has an air compressor plugged into the cigarette lighter that's airing up the front left tire. All four tires on the vehicle are bald, and the one he's pumping air into has a leak. "Is this the car in which we are about to drive through possible Russian-occupied territory?" I ask myself.

Shortly after we begin driving, we ask Otto to stop on the way to buy fresh flowers in case we meet Zac's birth mother. After a few more hours of driving on a winding dirt road, with God's assistance, we arrive at the village. As we approach, I notice the fertile fields that surround the area. Dozens of apple orchards are in view, none of them planted in straight rows. It appears they were all planted by hand. There are also wild plums growing everywhere. As I look around, a few Border Patrol trucks drive past us. They look different than the Border Patrol pickup trucks in Texas. While American Border Agents travel one or two agents at a time armed only with handguns, Georgian Border Patrol[36] drive army trucks labeled "Border Patrol" in English. Each truck is filled with troops armed with machine guns. As they drive by, I feel like every soldier is staring right at me. I notice that everyone I've seen in Georgia so far has a tan, black hair, and a nice jawline. They all look like my son Zac. From the back seat, Zac speaks as we pass the soldiers in trucks. "I could blend in here," Zac tells me. "But you look like a Russian." Knowing that we are close to a war zone, I don't feel relieved. This is not a good thing to look like when Georgian troops are fighting Russia a mile away, and I'm getting passed by the Border Patrol trucks.

For the past few miles, we have been traveling down dirt roads passing rubble and burned buildings that had been damaged during the Russian invasion five years ago. There is a donkey tied to a pole in front of a house standing on the dirt road. Our

---

36   http://bpg.gov.ge/en/land-border-defence

SUV edges past it with two wheels in the bar ditch on the side of the road. There are also chickens in the street. We continue to make our way through several small villages along this road. In most of the villages, the homes are enclosed with protective walls made of scraps of tin and stacked rubble. The farther we travel, the scarcer people are, and quieter are the streets.

When we get to the last village at the base of the mountains, there is a Y in the road. For a few minutes, we stop at the intersection. We are the only souls in sight. While we decide which path to take, a little old lady is walking down the road toward our car. Otto asks her if she knows where the Kristesiashvili family lives. This elderly woman says, "Well, I think a couple of villages back, there might be someone by that last name." The interpreter asks if she is sure there is no one else. She says, "No one else." Elza, the translator, asks her a third time and she says, "Wait a minute. There is a family by that name a block away from here if you take a left at this Y in the road."

We quickly pull over and park the car. Before any of us get out, Elza says, "This could have been a social disaster, a family disaster. You guys wait here, and I am going to walk down the road and see what I can find out." While Elza is walking alone down the dirt road, she sees only one person on the road. Elza asks the man, "Do you know anyone by the surname, Kristesiashvili?" The lone man on the road says, "Yes, that is us!"

Elza asks the man, "Do you know Lena?" He turns and calls his wife out of the house. His wife comes out to the street and starts talking to Elza. The two ladies walk back down the dirt road to where we are waiting. The woman walking with Elza looks like Zac with a wig and is wearing a bright colored dress. When she sees Zachary, she starts jabbering in Georgian. She puts her hands on Zac's face and kisses his cheeks. Then she looks at Zac and lets loose with another excited flurry of foreign words. I asked the interpreter what is going on. Elza says she will tell me later but explains this is Zac's birth-aunt, Nino. This continues for several minutes with Zac and I not included in the conversation.

Finally, Elza fills us in. We find out Zac's birth-mother lives two buildings down from where we ate dinner the night before in the capital city of Tbilisi. She also tells us that there were five sisters in the family and Nino is the youngest. In the entire country of Georgia, there are only two people that know about Zachary's birth; Nino and Zac's birth-mother, Lena. Zac's birth-mother is the fourth daughter of the family. Nino and her husband have only been married two years, and he does not know a lot of the family history. She had kept this family secret from her husband, her other sisters, and her mom and dad. Amazingly, she is willing to share this secret with us even though we are complete strangers. Especially when one of us, myself, looks like a Russian, their enemy.

After she calms, Nino tells us that years ago, a young lady was killed by her father for being pregnant out of wedlock in that same village at the time Zac was born. She would not explain the circumstances of Zac's birth and said that it was the birth mother's place to share what had happened. Many people in the village do not have cars, but Nino pulls a cell phone out. Most cell phones in Georgia are knockoff versions of American smartphones made in China. Quickly, she dials and calls Zachary's birth giver.

It's truly a miracle that we found one of only two people in Georgia who are aware of Zac's existence. Tbilisi has one million of the total 3.7 million Georgian population. The city is also incredibly ethnically diverse, meaning that not all its residents even speak the same language. They also don't make phone books in Tbilisi. The Soviet Union used to assign a family to an apartment, the family would live in or keep the apartment for life. For the most part, people stayed where they were assigned and never moved. We could not have found Nino or Lena on purpose; only the Holy Spirit could have led us to them.

After a quick back and forth, Nino tells us that Lena whose nickname is Lika wants to meet us. Nino explains to Elza that the birth giver is shocked that we are here. She also says that Lika has suffered from severe anxiety and has required medicine for anxiety. John 10:10 says, "The thief comes only to kill, steal and destroy, but I have come that you might have life and have it more abundantly." This woman's life has been on hold for 18 years. She has kept a secret, living in the capital city alone and away from her family for 18 years. She has never been married; never had any other children. All the other sisters are married. But God did not forget her. Jesus will leave the 99 and search for the 1. Matthew 18:2 and Luke 15:1-7 tell that story.

MIRACULOUS REUNION

We travel back to the capital to meet Lena. On the way, we pass Nada and Otto's apartment that we ate at the night before. Just a block away, we drive past the only medical school next door and park outside Lena's apartment. It's on the same street! The building is an old ugly Soviet concrete apartment building built in the 1940s. It's also badly in need of repair. As we enter the lobby, everything in it is pitch black. The electricity in the whole building seems to be off. All the lights are out, and the elevator doesn't work.

We decide to take the stairs. After walking up four flights, we knock on the door. A small, pretty woman dressed modestly in well-worn clothing answers. She is shaking. This is Zachary's birth mother, Lika.

As we enter her apartment, she immediately leads us to the living room. As we sit on the couch, the lights and electricity in the building turn back on! The first few minutes are very awkward. Neither Zachary nor Lika are talkers. They sit next to each other on the couch. Both of them are staring nervously forward. I end up doing most of the talking through Elza. We find out Lika has been unemployed for two months. She is 40 years old and likes the same things that Zachary does. Lika and Zac both do not like having their pictures taken. Lika enjoys playing tennis and swimming. A lone worn book with a faded cover is on the coffee table. It is the Adventures of Huckleberry Finn by Mark Twain; only this copy is in Georgian. She tells us that she

51

likes the book and has regularly read it over and over for entertainment. The apartment has only a few pictures on the wall. The paint is faded and chipped with sparse worn furnishings.

She asks if Zachary likes boiled corn. After trying to process the question (boiled corn is not something Zac is used to being offered), he shrugs and tells Elza yes. Lika goes to the kitchen and brings us two lukewarm ears of corn and places them in front of Zac and me. Elza explains that Lika had eaten yesterday and had saved this for her dinner tonight. She also takes the chocolate that we have brought her as a gift and poured them in a bowl for all of us. She also takes the coffee we bought for her as a gift to the kitchen and returns shortly after with fresh coffee for each of us. As she gives each of us our cup, her hands, and the saucers she's holding are both shaking. She is very nervous.

After a long conversation, we eventually reached an awkward pause. Elza asks us if there is anything else we would like to ask Lika. Zac asks about the circumstances of his birth. When Elza translates his question, tears start to run down Lika's cheeks. I didn't need an interpreter to see her anguish. She explained that she had just graduated from the nursing school in the capital city. She had been raised in the little village we have traveled to earlier before that. Her eyes were darting as she shared. She spoke in short bursts and sat stiffly on the edge of her seat as tears flowed. After moving to the big city, she had met a man and only knew him for a short time. He was not interested in staying with her in Tbilisi. The last she had heard, he left and moved to a war-torn province in the East where his family lived. Since then, she has never heard from or of him again. The country was in civil war and chaos. Otto chimed in and added that during that time, the country was a complete mess. Many people were literally starving, and organized crime syndicates ran the cities. Lena took several long silent pauses as she told her incredible story. Through the interpreter, I thanked Lena for being so brave to carry the pregnancy and give Zac a chance.

DISCUSSION QUESTIONS

- Does it matter what you say? What does the Bible say about the power of words? What makes some words more powerful than others? And does God intend to speak out of your mouth?

- Have you ever seen a miracle? Can you think of situations where a young person had hopes for their future derailed by the Devil? What does the Bible say concerning our part in their recovery?

- Are there family secrets that God wants to bring reconciliation and restoration to in your family? How can you cooperate with God in bringing reconciliation?

KEY TO SUCCESS

- Planning and organization are important, but God is not limited to our schedule of events. Ask God to make you aware of divine appointments that were not penciled in on your agenda.

• Help meet the practical needs of widows and orphans for food, safety, and clothing.

Never underestimate the power of listening. Sometimes all people need is for someone to care enough to hear their story.

(Above) Zac's aunt helped him reunite with his birthmother for the first time in seventeen years. Zac brought her flowers when he saw her the first time.

(Below) Richard, Lena, and Zac share a reunion toast with homemade Georgian Wine.

CHAPTER FOUR

HOPE INTERRUPTED

"For as many are led by the Spirit of God, they are the sons of God."   Romans 8:14 KJV

When Lika finished, I felt led to share the Good News about Jesus with her. After eight days of no opportunities to tell others the Good News, it felt right. As I began to share, Otto, who was our driver, and is Georgian Orthodox, loudly interjected. At first, I couldn't figure out what he was saying, but it wasn't good. I found out later he kept telling Lika, "They are not one of us! They don't think like we think." The louder Otto got, the more timid Lika became. I decided I would have to choose a different moment. There was no way I would successfully be able to speak over Otto.

I ask if Zac and I can pray a blessing over her. She smiles and nods. It was so clear she had carried the guilt and regret of giving Zac away by herself for 18 years. She needed healing, a divine encounter with the Redeemer so she could be free of the burden of shame she had lived under for so long. If not today, it would be soon. We were not leaving Georgia without Lika meeting Christ.

The end of our time together felt strained and had been made awkward. In the end, we promised her that we would bring her a Bible. She tells us that she has never had a Bible before; she is 40 years old and has never heard the good news of the Gospel. We let her know that we will come back before we go back to America.

Jesus says obstacles (offenses) are going to happen but woe to those who put obstacles (offenses) in front of the little ones.

While we are getting up to leave the apartment, fireworks begin to go off not far away. We end up having a perfect view from her small balcony. Otto guesses they are celebrating the first day of school. I left the apartment with an overwhelming burden to tell Lika about the Lord and am frustrated that I have to wait a few more days.

When we get back to the hotel, I head to the hotel room. Zac goes to the dining room. When I round the corner to the dining room, I am pleased to see Zac pouring out his story to Odd and Clyde at a dining table. They are the only ones in the room. I slip away unnoticed so that I don't interrupt.

On September 17, we start the day with breakfast at 9:00 a.m. The power struggle between the Orthodox Church, Russia, and the Georgian government that was explained to us earlier becomes more apparent. Helen tells us about her meeting with the former high-ranking leader the night before. He told her that due to a recent conflict he had with the current President of Georgia, he had recently nearly been thrown into prison. What saved him was his close friendship with the Patriarch of the Orthodox Church, who was able to convince the President not to. He ended up resigning from his post even though he was near retirement and by doing so forfeited his pension. He now works for the Russian company that provides electricity to the entire country. Helen added that most Georgians do not know that Russia still controls their electricity. He also questioned/ interrogated Helen concerning the future Billy Graham Crusade planned in Georgia as well as questioned the legitimacy of World Missions Alliance.

While we are on the hotel lobby balcony, Clyde tells me about his talk with Zac on the hotel roof. He explained that as they approached the edge of the balcony, he could tell Zac was a little bit timid. Zac asked him if Clyde was afraid of heights. Clyde said only slightly and that for most of his life he was. For a long time, he could not walk to the edge of a balcony like this because his knees would get weak. It wasn't until he was 35–40 years old that he worked up the courage to face his fear of heights.

Clyde also told Zac about his fear of public speaking and how he had also decided to face that fear as well, even if it meant embarrassing himself. When Clyde was in his 30s, he had planned an event for his church. A man in his 50s asked Clyde if he was going to call him out to speak if he came to the event. Clyde did end up calling the same man out to share with the crowd, which ended up helping the man overcome his fear. In telling

Zac his story, Clyde was hoping to help Zac overcome some of the same fears he had. Letting him know that if two older gentlemen could do it, Clyde was sure Zac could too.

Elza offered to arrange a meeting for Zac, myself, and Lika. I tell Elza that I believed Lika would not be able to meet that day but would be willing to meet the next day. Elza persists, I say give it a try. Elza is amazed that it happened just as I had told her it would.

Clyde, Zac, Elza and I go to the new mall at 4:30 p.m. I buy a shirt for the next day. We eventually travel up the mountain to get a closer look at the "Museum of the kings." I am struck by the unusual pillars at the base of the stairs leading up from a parking lot to the Stonehenge replica. I prayed that any ungodly influence would be dispossessed from this place in Jesus name and that everywhere my feet tread will be under the authority of the Kingdom of God.

CELEBRATION OF LIVES

The second to last night in Georgia, I have some trouble falling asleep. While praying and reading the Bible, God shows me what to share with Lika the next day.

On the last day of our stay in Georgia, we are scheduled to meet Lika again. Lika and Elza have been texting for two days. Elza tells me that Lika is excited and has bought presents to give to Zac. The scriptures say the Kingdom of Heaven suffers violence and the violent take it by force. Zac, Elza and I take a taxi from our hotel to Lika's apartment. In the cab, Zac hides money in the new Bible that we plan to give to Lika.

Once we entered her apartment, we could feel Lika's excitement. She was not the sad and withdrawn woman we had met just two days before. As we sit down on her couch, I tell her through the interpreter, "I may never see you again, and there is something God wants me to tell you." The night before the Lord showed me to show her John 3:1-17 and Romans 10:9. From the new Bible we give her, the interpreter reads John chapter 3. It's the story of Nicodemus, how even though Nicodemus was a God-fearing person, there was still something more he needed to do to get right with God. He needed to be born of the Spirit. After we finish, she tells us she has never heard this story before. That didn't surprise me. To explain to her how to be born of the Spirit, we read Romans 10:9 where it says, "Believe in your heart and confess with your mouth." I explained to her the significance of the verse. I asked her, "Do you want to accept this free gift of life that is being offered to you? Nobody can earn it, but you can accept it." She said, "Yes of course, who would not want to accept it?" She accepted Jesus on the last day of our trip.

The moment we prayed the sinner's prayer together, the atmosphere completely changed in the apartment. Only a few days ago, Zachary and Lika were complete strangers who just stared at each other. Lika was living under a crippling yoke of guilt and shame while Zac was living without a basic understanding of why or how he was born. Now, however, her cold and tiny apartment was filled with forgiveness, laughter, and joy. We were there for several hours, and she brought bowls of beans, salad, and corn on the cob which were from the hometown village. The raspberry jam was made by Aunt Nino, from the village. The bread was homemade. We had a feast!

Lika gave Zac the paintings she had bought the day before for him. It was obviously a big deal to her when she placed a gold chain around Zac's neck. She posed for pictures while doing so. Elza explained that it is an important tradition in Georgia to put gold jewelry on your child. Lika asked if we would like Georgian wine. I said sure. She comes around the corner with a reused liter plastic bottle with some dark homemade Georgian wine. It was delicious. After the meal, Lika asked if we wanted to take some wine home with us. I thought of the bottles exploding in my luggage at 30,000 feet in the air, -60° over Iceland while we are flying. Then I think about Houston being 88° and sea level. If the bottle had not exploded before, surely it would explode now due to the extreme changes in pressure and temperature. I also did not want any trouble while passing through US Customs. I politely turned her down, but she was insistent. She handed me two used one-liter plastic soft-drink bottles filled with home-made wine to take with me. As I mentioned earlier, Zachary never likes to have his picture taken. Throughout Zac's childhood, in half of Zac's pictures, he has his hand up hiding his face. I always say, "He is like Sasquatch,[37] hard to document with pictures!" I find out she is usually like that as well.

---

37   https://en.wikipedia.org/wiki/Bigfoot

Tonight is a special night for all of us. You can feel it in the air. Zac and Lika pull their cameras out, and they are taking pictures of each other. They ask me to take pictures of them as well. We have pictures of Zac taking pictures of Lika taking pictures of Zac! This is not normal! This is a new thing. Our God is a Redeemer, and I am convinced that her future is to be the woman at the well who goes back to her village and tells them what Jesus has done for her and brings the Good News of the Gospel to the whole village.

It was the 11th hour when we shared the good news with Lika. We say goodbye and start to walk out of Lika's apartment when fireworks start to go off outside her balcony! We stop to watch the fireworks. It was a perfect night.

I need one more miracle. I have the liter bottles of homemade Georgian wine, and I am going to put them in my luggage, and it is going to go 30,000 feet in the air at -60°. When you are flying on a commercial airliner, they often tell you how cold it is outside and how high you are in the air. The monitor also shows you a map of where you are on your trip. Later, Clyde and I pray at the Georgian airport for the plastic bottles of wine to make it home, intact and trouble free through customs.

Before we take off to Germany, I buy some honey at the airport in Georgia. I thought that would be neat to have, a small souvenir from our trip. As we pass through customs in Germany, they confiscate the honey but do not take the wine. Clyde says, "You know you are supposed to have that wine for your ceremony with Zac." When I get home, Danny Skaggs explains that the wine is meant to be used in communion during your ceremony. The wine made it; I don't know how; it is one more miracle.

On September 21, a few days after we get home, we receive an email from Elza. She writes,

"Hello, Mr. Richard and Zac! How are you doing? I've missed you when you left. How did you make it back home? Is everything ok there? I have good news; Zac's birth mother called me and asked me to visit her. Since you left, she has called me twice, asking if you got back safe. Tomorrow after church, I'm planning to visit her. I hope I'll get more opportunity to talk to her about the Lord and God's ways. This entire story is a miracle for me! I'm really thankful to you that you allow me to be part of it. God showed me a lot of things through this..."

Two days later, she writes to us again...

"Thank you very much for your reply. Yesterday I went to Lika. She was very glad to see me; she asked a lot about you. Even things she already was told. I think she was very much on emotions those days and she didn't remember it all. She said to me that she forgot that day to invite your family to Georgia. She said if your family decides to visit her sometime in the future, she will be very happy and will tell her relatives about Zac and his story. She invited me to her village to get to know her family better."

DISCUSSION QUESTIONS

- What Bible stories tell of a temporary change in someone's personality for the better? What evidence of the change is recorded?

- Does the Great Commission apply to you? What is your part today?

- Have you ever had a good thing God wanted you to do that got interrupted? What does the Bible say about that?

- Have you ever led someone to Jesus for salvation? Why or why not?

KEY TO SUCCESS

- If you stay faithful, God will open up the proper doors in His timing.

- To quote Pastor Tim Storey: "Never forget that someone is always waiting for you on the other side of your obedience."

- Have Faith that God is a miracle working God.

Georgian Orthodox Churches in Tbilisi

Despite Economic hardship, the Republic of Georgia decreed that all public buildings must be modern and of original design.

Zac stands on the steps of a monastery a few hours before the miraculous reunion with his birth mother.

Bershueti, Georgia

In the midst of the war between Georgia and Russia, life on the border between these two countries reveals the spiritual oppression which is evident.

Zac stand by a memorial to the Georgian soldiers who fought against Russia in the 2008 war.

(Above) War Memorial commemorating the Georgian-Russian 2008 War.

(Below) Memorial honoring the past Georgian Orthodox Priests.

Richard and Ben Bartlett at the Medical Clinic during the Guatemala Mission Trip

Building A New Church Building in Guatemala

Ben Bartlett mixes concrete by hand

Common sights in Guatemala on the 2014 mission trip

Yezidi Refugee Camp

Yezidi Refugee Camp

Yezidi Children in the Refugee Camp – Many made orphans by ISIS

Christians distribute food and supplies to the Yezidi refugees.

Christians distribute food and supplies to the Yezidi refugees.

Yezidi at the Refugee Camp

Medical Clinic in small Yezidi refugee tent.

Medical Clinic in small Yezidi refugee tent.

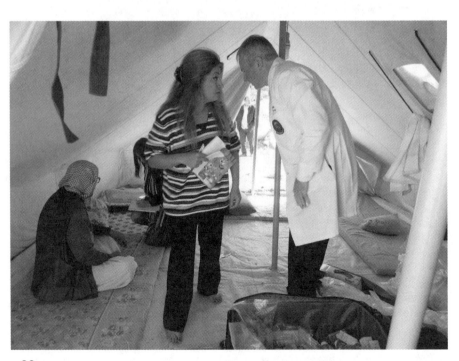

(Above) Dr. Bartlett invites the Kurdish commander
and soldier to the church service after the clinic.

(Below) Commander meets Rev. Chuck Todd at the evening church service.

(Above) Young lady who was murdered in Mosul. Her mother forgave the unforgivable with God's grace.

(Below) Cancer patient said that she heard God say He would grant any request the mission team prayed.

Daniel lures Muslim children out of hiding to play soccer and forget the fear of ISIS.

Mission Team on mountain overlooking Mosul, praying for God to deliver the Kurds from ISIS.

Our team landed in Erbil and then drove to Dohuk which is 30 miles from Mosul. The road forced us to journey within 12 miles of Mosul which at the time was the headquarters of ISIS.

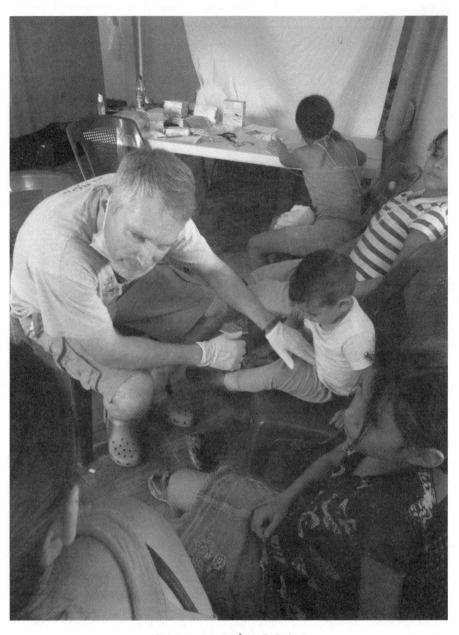

Guatemala 2014

Medical clinic in church. Dr. Bartlett joined Crossroads Fellowship of Odessa, TX mission trip.

CHAPTER FIVE

CROSSROADS IN GUATEMALA

"Then Jesus came to them and said, "All authority in heaven and on earth has been given to me. Therefore go and make disciples of all nations, baptizing them in the name of the Father and of the Son and of the Holy Spirit, and teaching them to obey everything I have commanded you. And surely I am with you always, to the very end of the age."   *Matthew 28:18-20 NIV*

Ben and I went to Guatemala[38] for a seven-day mission trip with Crossroads Fellowship Church in November 2013. There were four goals for the mission team. The first one would be overseen by myself and Dr. Smith who was an ophthalmologist. Together, we would open up a free medical clinic that would operate out of two different churches. Several other men who were mechanics would repair and service vehi-

---

38   https://en.wikipedia.org/wiki/Guatemala

cles for the local pastors and missionaries. The women who were going would help each church put on a Vacation Bible School for kids. Finally, one church was building an outdoor kitchen and also needed a new coat of paint outside. These Christians excelled in showing God's love through good works.

As we flew into Guatemala City[39] at night, we could see the lights of the city and surrounding communities snaking up and down the mountains. Storm clouds on the edge of the city were lighting up with lightning. Ben and I were seated in the last row by the window. Another jet that was headed straight from the back of our plane passed by dangerously close to us.

The first two days of the medical clinic were in the church of an impoverished Pacific coast town of La Gomera. During day one of operating our medical clinic, I told the Good News of the Gospel to every patient I treated. Through the nurse who was also my interpreter, I led six people in prayer through receiving Jesus as their Savior. On the second day of the clinic, eight people prayed the sinner's prayer in the same way. We also visited a family in their home. Before I got there, the mother told me that her house had dirt floors. When I got there, I was saddened to see this dear family with five children living in such a poorly constructed shelter. Their home was comprised of black plastic draped over sticks and boards held together by string and twine. The outdoor toilet was a toilet over a hole in the dirt with a trench leading out of a similar tiny structure with black plastic. Fellow Christians were barely surviving.

---

39   https://en.wikipedia.org/wiki/Guatemala_City

The last two days of the medical clinic were in a different church on the edge of Guatemala City. Ten people prayed with me to receive Christ in the clinic on the third day. At the end of that day, I walked out of the church to stand by myself next to our van in the alleyway. As I stood, I noticed a young drunk man pressing the elderly pastor for food at the gate of the church. The older pastor had suffered a previous heart attack and stroke. Despite the pastor's best efforts to suggest the man to leave, he continued to press. Quickly, I got an interpreter and told the drunken man the Good News. With tears flowing down his face, he repeated after the interpreter as he prayed to receive Christ and ask God for freedom from drug and alcohol abuse. The nurses brought him leftover sandwiches from our lunch earlier that day. He promised to return to the church with his sons for the next service.

On the last day of the clinic, 20 people prayed to receive Christ as their savior. After the clinic, I again went to the alley to stand by the van. A mother carrying her sick baby came to me. It was evident that she had come for help too late and was turned away. Regardless, I led her inside and cared for the baby. I shared the Good News with the mother, and she prayed to receive Jesus as her Savior.

We prayed for the sick as we shared the Gospel of Christ. At one point, when Dr. Smith was examining an 87-year-old lady, he noticed she had evidence of a severe cardiovascular problem. After his discovery, he asked me to examine her as well. After my examination, we shared the Gospel with her, and she received

Christ. Dr. Smith had brought a significant amount of reading glasses to dispense. After the last day of the clinic, several older men came in asking for reading glasses even though they had not been seen in the clinic before. Through an interpreter, one of the men repeated the prayer inviting Christ to be his Lord and Savior.

A mother brought her three daughters to the medical clinic. They all had abdominal discomfort as did almost everyone we saw in Guatemala. During the clinic visit, I started to tell the Good News through the interpreter. The mother began to knowingly nod her head as if to dismiss the topic explaining that her family already attended this church. I felt the need to ask her not to answer for her daughters. I individually asked them if they had asked Jesus to come into their hearts. Each one thoughtfully listened and said one by one that they had not but that they wanted to accept Jesus. They all repeated after the interpreter as they were led in prayer to receive forgiveness for all mistakes and to ask Jesus to come into their hearts and to be in charge of their lives. It was a reminder that Jesus has a personal relationship with each follower. No spouse or parent can answer for another person. Each person must decide to follow Jesus on their own. God has sons and daughters, not grandkids by faith.

Several of the people I met stood out to me. America is a 39-year-old single mother who came for medical care. She gladly accepted Christ as her savior. She left the church to retrieve her teenage daughter so I could tell her the Gospel. The daughter was already a Christian and attended this church regularly.

America had one other daughter, and she wanted her to hear the Good News as well. Thirty minutes later, she returned from home with the second daughter. She had already accepted Christ and also regularly attended this church. She reminded me of the woman at the well who wanted to tell others about the Jesus she now knew.

Another patient was four months pregnant and was accompanied by her grade-school-age son and daughter. She was soft-spoken, and one of her eyes was discolored and blind. She was seeking help because of a vaginal discharge she had had since before the pregnancy. On questioning, she said she knew her husband had a lifestyle of adultery. We treated her for venereal disease and also prayed for her and her family. After telling her the Good News, she also received Christ as her savior.

A 55-year-old man who worked as a laborer came in because he sometimes had back pain, though he did not have pain at the time of the clinic visit. He also prayed to receive Christ as his savior. Almost all of the people I met were humble and willing to receive help from man or God. After sharing the Good News with one lady, she said she did not want to give up her religion. She was Catholic, and although she had never asked Jesus into her life or heard the Gospel before we presented it, she was fearful to let go of the familiar. After further explanation, she prayed to receive Christ as her Lord and Savior. Very few said no thank you.

Back at the Manna House that was our lodging, several men on the mission's trip stayed up late to talk in the living room.

One man shared how he had a lifestyle of adultery and had abandoned his family several years ago. Over the last 25 years, he went on yearly mission trips interestingly. He became suicidal and had a near-death experience driving over a bridge head-on into a truck. He could not explain how the accident did not occur. Shortly after that, he started having flashbacks of his younger years. He realized, for the first time that he had been raped as a 5-year-old boy by an uncle in the Baptist church; he would later accept Christ as his savior in that same church.

We prayed for generational curses to be broken from his life and for healing. Another man on the mission's team shared how his father abandoned his pregnant mother. Growing up, he would hear reports that his father would come to the town he and his mother lived in, but would never visit him. With tears flowing, he expressed he was fearful that he would follow in his father's footsteps. We prayed that God would break generational curses and that he would be free in Christ. They both volunteered the following day that they literally felt different and were very thankful.

MINISTER WHERE YOU LIVE

As I returned home to Texas from Guatemala, I wondered if leading people to receive Christ would decrease. The following Monday, 20 out of the 43 men that came to my office, prayed with me to receive Christ as their savior. I have had people from all over the world come to my office and pray to receive Christ as their Lord and Savior. A Tongan man, from the Pacific Islands who worked for years on container ships, was applying for his first job in the US. Other people had attended Baptist churches for years but made the commitment to accept Christ for the first time in my office. Some were recently out of prison but open to Christ. A 53-year-old man named John Wayne said he had heard the Good News many times but had not accepted Christ. He chose to pray and accept Christ the day I presented the Gospel.

Very few were anti-Christ. I shared the Good News in my medical clinic on different occasions with two Muslims and one practicing Wicca witch. We were able to have peaceful conversations even though they did not accept Christ at the time. I remember one young man from Louisiana who said he did not want to receive Christ. When asked, he explained that he liked to earn everything in his life. There was a block to reasoning with him, but he was not hostile.

On December 6, 2013, we held the rite of passage ceremony for my son Zac. Odd and Elise Frustol flew from their home in New Jersey to join us in Texas for the event. Close friends of mine that I pray with regularly were invited to participate as well. Danny and Kara Skaggs offered their newly renovated home for the ceremony. The homemade Georgian wine was used in the communion taken at the rite of passage event. Framed pictures of our trip to Georgia were displayed in the living room during the ceremony. A professional photographer recorded everything.

Every week I continue to have the privilege of leading strangers to Jesus Christ and then leading them in prayer to receive Christ as Lord and Savior. The Bible says, "A man is snared by the words of his mouth." And, "Ask and you shall receive." Also, "If you believe with your heart and confess with your mouth, Jesus Christ is Lord, you will be saved."

In Midland, I ask the X-ray tech, Raquel, to interpret as I share the Good News with a gentleman who only spoke Spanish. The man prayed to accept Jesus as his Lord and Savior. Later that day, the X-ray technician interpreted again as I shared the Good News with a patient and his wife. They prayed to receive Jesus as well. Thirty minutes later, I asked the X-ray tech if she wanted to receive Jesus. She quickly teared up and said yes. I was so excited that people were being saved from hell and brought into new life with Jesus.

When I would tell some Christians of new converts accepting the Lord, I was surprised that their first response was not praise or thanksgiving to God but "Who is going to follow up with them?" My response would be that I am the messenger of the Good News of the Gospel and God is the provider and teacher. In the Bible, God says: "Great is the peace of My children and they are instructed by the Lord." Evidence of this reality is Raquel the X-Ray tech. Raquel sent me a text several weeks after she accepted Jesus into her heart. She said that she had been invited to a Bible study and she felt like it was God's hand that came upon her when we prayed together and eventually led her to the Bible study. The Holy Spirit coordinated the follow-up.

On December 28, 2013, Eva Perrin gave this prophecy after we all took communion together in my living room. "Richard and Dawn are like palm trees giving shelter to many in the past and future." Eva had a vision of us sitting on a plane holding drinks with little umbrellas. "You will travel the world and bring shelter to many. Multiplication, to give to others, but also for your dreams to come true. Dawn, God knows how you think and will give you the desires of your heart, your special ministry/purpose/business."

When she is done, Eva reads Deuteronomy 11:8-12 —

The essence was that God is bringing us into a place in time where He will personally watch over and provide for the harvest from the beginning of the year to the end.

DISCUSSION QUESTIONS

- Do you have a spiritual testimony? Have you shared it?
- What does the Bible say about a personal spiritual testimony?
- What are generational curses and iniquities of forefathers and how does the Bible instruct you to deal with them?
- What does the Bible teach about Good Works?

KEY TO SUCCESS

- Share the Best News Ever with people as the Holy Spirit leads you.
- Pray for needs, don't just talk about them.
- Trust in the Lord with all your heart, mind, and soul.

Kurdistan Flag on the mountainside above the city of Duhok, Iraq. Duhok is 30 miles from Mosul which was the headquarters of ISIS at time of this photo.

The picture of the flag on the mountainside, which is magnified in the insert, was a statement of defiance against ISIS and anyone who would take independence away from the Kurdish people.

CHAPTER SIX

OPEN DOORS IN KURDISTAN

"He will call on Me, and I will answer him; I will be with him in trouble, I will deliver him and honor him."   *Psalm 91:15 NIV*

In February 2014, Chuck returned home from a mission to Kurdistan. I called him to hear about the trip. His mission team went to a refugee camp that was designed to take care of 30,000 people, but because of terror threats, it had been overrun and currently supported 70,000 refugees. While Chuck was there, he was able to go in and out of the refugee camp, meet with people, then come and go as he pleased. The usual rules that applied to U.N.-supported refugee camps did not seem to apply to him or his team. It was an open door from the Lord to go in and share the Gospel. Chuck told me they were planning another trip in November so they would not miss the opportunity to continue to preach the gospel. I told him I wanted to go to Kurdistan and run a medical clinic with him and his team. When he explained that he did not know how to do that, I told him I would handle the medical part if he would do the rest.

Danny Skaggs, a friend of mine who owns a pharmacy in Odessa, Texas, wanted to donate the medication for the mission trip. I made a list of what I needed, and although he thought there was no way I was going to use them all, he got it all together and had it specially packaged. It was so much to take I had to pack it in two huge duffle bags and a big suitcase to carry it all with me to Kurdistan.

We bought the tickets early in the year. I planned on taking my third son, Daniel, who was seventeen years old at the time. I had taken international father-son trips with each of his older brothers over the last two years, and it was his turn this time. This was the first year we home-schooled Daniel which freed him up to travel in November.

ISIS

June 2014, ISIS[40] first appears in the news. They are a terrorist group who behead women and children, sell others as sex slaves, and crucify Christians. Their newly declared nation is in Syria and Iraq. The extreme brutality and wickedness of ISIS appeared to be escalating every passing month. Mosul[41] is the city of Nineveh[42] in the Bible. One of the first things ISIS did after

---

40   http://www.bbc.com/news/world-middle-east-29052144
41   https://en.wikipedia.org/wiki/Mosul
42   https://www.britannica.com/place/Nineveh-ancient-city-Iraq

they had conquered Mosul was to desecrate the bones and grave of Jonah.[43] I did not know anyone even knew where the grave of Jonah was until it made international news on CNN. All the things I learned about in the Bible were being substantiated in the evening news.

The national news was reporting ISIS atrocities mainly in Syria. I tried to decrease my wife's concerns by pointing out they were not very active in Iraq.

On August 8, 2014, I took my wife to France for the first time. We toured the country with some dear friends, Carl and Carrie Britton, who had been in France before. We returned to the US via the Newark airport. As we slowly made our way through the crowded customs line, all the ceiling mounted monitors were covering CNN's Breaking News. ISIS had surrounded Kurds on a mountain, Sinjar,[44] in northern Iraq. Anderson Cooper was the anchorman who explained that the Kurds in this region were of an ancient religion called the Yazidi.[45] Cooper implied that the Yazidi are like Christians in that they believe in one God and Noah's Ark. It was obvious he was leading the world to believe they were similar to Christians. Cooper said it was an impending genocide[46] and that world leaders were calling for Obama to intervene.[47] Carl and Carrie looked at each

---

43 https://lifehopeandtruth.com/bible/holy-bible/old-testament/the-prophets/minor-prophets/jonah/

44 https://en.wikipedia.org/wiki/Sinjar_massacre

45 http://religion.oxfordre.com/view/10.1093/acrefore/9780199340378.001.0001/acrefore-9780199340378-e-254

46 https://en.wikipedia.org/wiki/Genocide_of_Yazidis_by_ISIL

47 https://www.nytimes.com/2014/08/08/world/middleeast/obama-weighs-military-strikes-to-aid-trapped-iraqis-officials-say.html

other in silence. Despite being worried about me, they didn't say anything discouraging. Dawn was silent as well. The whole experience was surreal. That said, instead of discouraging me, it steeled my resolve that I was called to go to Iraq. I could not explain it logically.

The plight of the siege on Sinjar Mountain was the focus of news around the world during the following days. The whole world looked to the United States to intervene. President Obama dropped water and some food on the mountain. Due to mounting international pressure, he finally bombed the ISIS terrorists, and the Yazidi ran from the mountain for their lives across the desert with just the clothes on their backs. Little did I know I would be caring for these very people months later.

I had a lot of family and friends that had legitimate concerns about me going to Kurdistan. Some even tried to talk me out of going. It is a real gut check to see if you are doing the right thing when your 5-year-old son is crying and begging you not to go. The thing is, when God puts something in your spirit, the call does not go away.

I called Chuck to review our plans. He told me we would have military escorts and that the trip was still on. Over the next few days, I did some serious soul-searching. "I am fifty years old," I thought. "How old do I have to be to entrust my life and my family's welfare to the Lord and follow Him into danger. There are eighteen-year-old young men and women who put their lives on the line in the military every day. Certainly, I can stand up for an even greater cause."

In September 2014, I volunteered to be the flight doctor for the first Honor Flight from the Permian Basin. Honor Flight[48] is a non-profit organization that has been taking veterans from different parts of the US to Washington DC for years. The three-day journey is packed with wreath-placing ceremonies at the various war memorials, bagpipes, trumpets playing Taps, and gun salutes at Arlington Memorial Cemetery. The purpose is to honor the veterans. During the trip, many tears are shed. Stories that have never been told are shared for the first time. It was truly an honor to be a part of the process of establishing this worthy program in West Texas. My goal was to give honor where honor is due. Little did I know God would use the Honor Flight to speak to me.

BLACKHAWKS & MARINES

Four signs encouraged me and let me know that God's favor was on the trip and confirmed that I was supposed to go to Kurdistan. The first sign came in the form of receiving support with a Blackhawk helicopter pilot who offered to help me if I needed help or felt I was in danger on my trip. We met in September 2014 in Washington DC while I was on the Inaugural Honor Flight from Midland, Texas. I was the flight doctor and therefore charged to care for the WW2, Korean War, and Vietnam War veterans during the trip.

A Vietnam veteran, Rey Martinez, seated next to me on the tour bus heard about my upcoming trip to Northern Iraq. I

---

48   https://www.honorflight.org/

instantly had a friend. Rey said his brother, Fred, was a Black Hawk helicopter pilot who was shot down behind enemy lines at night. Armor piercing rounds had struck some control panels, forcing him to make an emergency landing. Even though he was shot down, Fred was able to repair the helicopter and land at the US base three hours later. His commanders asked how he did it. For, it had never been done before in the history of the US military.

Later on, Fred was hired by the company that makes Blackhawks as an advisor. Years later, these two brothers had made several inventions that had been incorporated in Blackhawks, and one invention that is now used on Air Force One. Fred still loved to fly military missions as a 'contractor.' Rey gave me his brother's number. Rey explained that Fred had relationships with powerful people in the Department of Defense and his company. He also told me that he would tell his brother Fred about me. He was confident his brother could help me if I ran into trouble.

When I returned home after the Honor flight, I called decorated Blackhawk pilot, Fred Martinez. Fred explained that his brother, Rey, had told him about me. He said that North Iraq was a war zone and that the Kurds were very honorable and would give their lives to protect me. He also told me that the US had people embedded in the area.

In fact, he was scheduled to do a "contractor mission" in Afghanistan at the time I would be in Iraq/Kurdistan. He said if I needed help, I could call him 24/7. If he couldn't help me, he would coordinate with someone else to help. He asked if he could pray for my safety at the end of our conversation. What a blessing!

The second sign was, on the same trip, I had the favor of an unexpected meeting with Senator Cornyn at a veteran's photo op in the rotunda of the Capital. That does not happen to me every day. I have never before had the honor of a US Senator seeking me out in the rotunda of the US capitol, to speak to me about anything! The retired Naval Master Sergeant in charge of the Honor Flight trip escorted Senator Cornyn across the crowded Capitol rotunda to discuss my upcoming trip in front of everyone. As the US Senator came closer to me, the CBS news camera crew came to life. The cameras were rolling in our faces with the lights glaring. The flashes from the newspaper cameras were blinding. At the moment, I was totally surprised. Senator Cornyn offered his hand for a handshake with a big smile. The Master Sarge told him I was going to do Humanitarian Care in Iraq. I was excited to explain that I was going to do free medical clinics for the victims of ISIS in Kurdistan. Senator Cornyn's brow furrowed as he explained how he didn't agree with President Obama's policies in Iraq. He slowly and deliberately said things are "dicey" in North Iraq right now. He started to say, "The King of Saudi Arabia says…" I cut him off mid-sentence saying, "My confidence is not in the King of Saudi Arabia. My confidence is in God." I have great respect for the Senator, but it just welled up and overflowed out of my spirit and out of my mouth.

My third sign came through a prophetic pastor, Tim Storey, who has a church in Orange County. He was a guest speaker in the nearby town of Big Spring,[49] Texas a week before my trip to Kurdistan. We went to Family Faith Center in Big Spring, Texas because Tim was teaching at the 10:00 a.m. service. We got to meet the regular pastors Sam and Jessica Segundo. After the service, they invited us to eat lunch with them and Tim. They prayed for us and then Tim put his hand on my son Daniel's chest and said "an impartation."

Tim then turned to me and said, "Doctor, the Lord needs you to do more as a physician. God has creative ideas for you and your family. God says creative ideas are from Him. He is going to give you inventions and ideas that are amazing, and they are going to bring wealth to your family and wealth into the Kingdom. And thank the Lord for the well. That is what the Lord showed me. There is a well in your soul for healing and miracles. You have studied and you have been interceding, and the Lord would say, even on this trip you will see from that well that you have, from that reservoir that many will be healed and the Presence will be heavy.

"The Lord would say to you that I have put ministering angels with you on this trip. You will even notice at times, that your angels are around you. There will be times that you will feel like you have bumped into an angel. And the Lord says to you, that is Him, that is God; He has put ministering angels around you. It is like hot oil about to go through your body right now.

49 https://en.wikipedia.org/wiki/Big_Spring,_Texas

We thank you Lord for a shield around both of them and their team. We thank you Lord for divine anointing that is unusual, very unusual. Breathe that in, oil of God through you, protection of God. Everybody lift your hands, it is very heavy in here and say, 'Father, we receive your healing into our lives, we receive sudden good breaks, financially, physically and for our families, and for this church.' You feel the level of this, if I didn't have a phone appointment I would stay, but I have to go."

Pastor Sam said to me, "I want you to look up the word **impervious** and take that with you. Google the word impervious. It means non-penetrable, nothing will touch you."

I said, "That's my word for the trip."

Pastor Sam Segundo said, "Nice."

Merriam-Webster says the word impervious means: not allowing something to enter or pass through, not bothered or affected by something.

My fourth sign was that a good friend, Jaime Gaona, who had retired from the Marines after 18 years, was asked to join the Blackwater contractors in a mission in North Iraq and was scheduled to arrive there a day before my trip. I felt this was a sign because I don't see Jamie for years at a time and here he was going to the same place as I was at the same time.

DISCUSSION QUESTIONS

- What is the difference between omens vs. signs from God? What does the Bible say about how God confirms His messages to you?

- What are some situations in your life where it is "to live is Christ, to die is gain?"

- Have you seen examples of sowing honor and reaping honor or vice versa? What does the Bible teach about honor?

- What is your main source of the truth (the Bible or the media?)

KEY TO SUCCESS

- God gives seed to the sower. The more willing you are for God to use you the more He will ask of you.

- As Christians, we do not live off of bread alone but every word that comes from the mouth of God.

When you decide to follow the call over your life, God will bring the right people around you to support you.

Medical Team in northern Iraq.

We did not look like Navy SEALs ready to take on ISIS.

CHAPTER SEVEN

PREPARING THE HOMESTEAD

*"No weapon forged against you will prevail, and
you will refute every tongue that accuses you.
This is the heritage of the servants of the Lord,
and this is their vindication from Me," declares
the Lord."*   Isaiah 54:17 NIV

I wanted to have my house in order before I left the country,
so my wife and I met with a friend who is an attorney, Wade
Hudman. I asked Wade to get my will in order. Several days
later, my wife called the insurance agent to see if my life insurance covered me on an international trip. The secretary assured
Dawn that, of course, I was covered on an international trip.
"That said," she continued, "he's not going somewhere crazy like
Iraq, right?" Dawn answered, "Actually, he is…" The secretary
responded, "I'll have to check and get back with you."

I had an excitement and expectation of God's protection on

this trip. Helen Todd explained that a nurse from Canada was going to join WMA on the WMA mission to the Republic of Georgia and then three days later continue with WMA to Kurdistan. The two countries are in the same region. I decided that was a good idea. My son and I would do the same. My wife, who is always understanding, said, "You know, it's going to be kind of like you're in a holding pattern in Georgia before you go to Kurdistan because really your heart's there with the Kurds." She was right; I felt called by God specifically to help the Kurds.

CBS and NBC are the top networks in West Texas. Both got wind of the upcoming trip to Iraq. Chuck and Helen Todd were speaking at Parker Heights Church in Odessa. Both TV crews showed up before the church service and recorded the entire service. They then recorded multiple interviews of Chuck and Helen, and my wife and I. Chuck explained how the Kurds are American allies and how they are standing up to ISIS against all the odds. I explained our plans to offer free medical care at our clinics.

Before Daniel and I left, we prayed as a family. "If it were me, you would not want me to go," Dawn said. She was right. She had a point. Dawn wasn't the only spouse feeling the gravity of the trip. Helen had also revealed one of her motives for going. If something were to happen to Chuck, she would rather endure the same fate as her husband. Chuck has a saying, "God tells us to go, but He doesn't always say we will come back."

YAZIDI RELIGION

While Daniel and I were in the Republic of Georgia, a voice woke me up in the middle of the night. I could clearly hear the voice say "Nahum." I looked at Daniel who was still in his bed sleeping. Not being able to shake what I heard, I got up and using the Bible App on my iPhone, began to read the first chapter of Nahum. The book talked about how God was an avenging God, and that He was going to judge the evil invaders of Nineveh. As it turns out, Nineveh is the ancient name of the city of Mosul, which is a very strategically important city located on the border of Iraq and Kurdistan. At the time, I did not know that was where ISIS's main headquarters was located. For, we were still in Georgia and had not made that second part of the trip yet. However, as I read in Nahum after God's judgment lands on Nineveh, He also judges someone who is there that is conspiring evil as well as sends the Good News on the heels of the judgment.

While Daniel and I are in Georgia, we meet with three pastors. Two of the pastors are Georgian, and one, a Kurdish pastor named Rezo, was previously of the Yazidi religion and had converted to Christianity. Due to the Kurds not having a country of their own for centuries, they can be found living all over the world—just like how the Jews did not have their own country until the 1940s. There are millions of Kurds living in Georgia. Just like the Americans, Georgians are religiously very diverse. The Kurdish people, in particular, adhere to many different religions. Even though Islam is the dominant tradition, many of them do not know much about the Koran or what it teaches.

Outside of Islam, another predominantly Kurdish religious group are the Yazidis. We had several encounters with Yazidis in Kurdistan. Pastor Rezo, who my son and I met in the Republic of Georgia, explained to us their beliefs. They believe in one God, the Creator, who is a kind God and doesn't hurt anybody. They also believe in a fallen archangel who is dangerous and hurts people often. Yazidis are taught to worship (out of fear) this fallen archangel, named Shaytan or Tawsi Melek, the Peacock Angel,[50] in hopes he won't hurt them. This has been the central religious story they have adhered to for thousands of years. A saying we have in Texas is "as proud as a peacock." Pride was a notable quality of Satan.

The 50,000 Bibles that were printed in the Kurdish dialect of Kurmanji[51] were in the Republic of Georgia, and our team helped strategize how to carry those to Kurdistan. A lot of the Kurds were in refugee camps on the Syrian-Turkish border and happened to speak the Kurmanji dialect of the WMA Bibles. Helen Todd, co-founder of World Missions Alliance, gave the bibles to Pastor Rezo in the Republic of Georgia to bring to the people in the refugee camp. Pastor Rezo said the refugees were wide open to the Good News of the Gospel. He was so excited that he started crying when he saw the Bibles.

---

50   https://en.wikipedia.org/wiki/Melek_Taus
51   https://en.wikipedia.org/wiki/Northern_Kurdish

We were also invited to speak at his Kurdish Christian Church in Georgia. Strange sounds filled the air as the Kurdish Christian worship team played instruments I had never seen before with an accompanying keyboard. The rhythm and beats were unusual to my American ears. I was not in Texas anymore! What was in store for us on the next leg of the trip in Iraq?

ISIS vs. KURDS

On November 3, 2014, Daniel and I left the Republic of Georgia and headed to Kurdistan. The first leg of our trip was a 3-hour flight from Tbilisi, Georgia to Ankara,[52] Turkey. After a quick stint on the tarmac, we took off again for Erbil,[53] the capital city of Kurdistan, 220 miles north of Baghdad. The day's trip took place at night. From my window seat, I could only see a few lights even though the population of Erbil was over a million.

Danger was in the air from the moment we landed in Erbil. The new airport facility had a similar design to the airport in Austin, Texas. The difference was this airport was operating with only a skeleton crew. The passengers from our plane were the only ones in the entire airport. As we waited for our luggage to appear on the conveyer, we noticed more people that were obviously on our mission team. Most passengers were not talking, but when someone did, it was in a hushed voice. Everyone appeared cautious and unusually alert despite the early morning hour, undoubtedly because we were in a war zone.

---

52 https://en.wikipedia.org/wiki/Ankara
53 https://en.wikipedia.org/wiki/Erbil

Our team gathered in a waiting area as Chuck Todd started to brief the team. Chuck explained that his original plan for us to travel at 4:00 a.m. across the desert to Erbil in the dark. However, things had changed. Barbara, a member of the team, had a flight connection that did not occur, so she was coming in later than expected.

Once I heard the news, I was relieved. I found out later that I was not the only team member who had a bad feeling about the cancelled night journey across the ISIS war zone. During several phone conversations before our trip, Chuck had tried to decrease my concern, assuring me that we would be traveling with a military detail and that terrorists usually don't fight as much in the pre-dawn hours.

As the sun started to rise, I could see the cranes and frames of new skyscrapers that were being erected. At that point, I could see no evidence of war from the airport waiting area.

Eventually, Barbara arrived after dawn. Once she got her luggage, we all piled into two white mini-vans with our luggage and gear secured on top. I saw few cars on the streets as we drove through the metropolitan downtown and toward the desert onto Mosul highway. The flat, arid, barren landscape appeared similar to West Texas. We started to pass fleets of brand new oilfield trucks. Again, a familiar sight.

Not far out of the city, we approached a military checkpoint. Five Kurdish soldiers with machine guns surrounded our mini-vans. They asked the driver for our passports. The driver explained that we had come to provide humanitarian aid from the U.S. Luck would have it that the first passport the soldier opened was Canadian! I couldn't help but laugh at how funny mini-vans full of mostly senior citizens passing through a war zone must have seemed to these battle-hardened soldiers. We definitely did not look like Navy Seals. We clearly did not pose a security threat.

As we drove away from the first checkpoint, the vastness of the Iraq desert swallowed all signs of civilization in our rear view. For the next 30 miles, we went through two more checkpoints and remnants of small villages that showed evidence of war.

We came to a crossroads on the edge of another small abandoned village. The driver told us it was critical we did not miss this turn, or we would drive 10 miles right into the arms of ISIS in Mosul. I would later find out that Abu Bakr Al-Baghdadi,[54] the founder of ISIS was in Mosul at that time.

After turning North, the mountains appeared on the horizon. Chuck explained the Kurds had a saying, "We may not have friends, but at least we have the mountains." The Kurds had repeatedly used the mountains as a place of refuge during times of persecution. Whether it was Saddam or ISIS, when things got tough, the Kurds got to the mountains.

The Kurdish saying stayed with me for the rest of our journey through the rugged mountains. As we drove, random abandoned homes would appear in the distance that had been damaged by war. Eventually, we crested a final mountain and found ourselves

---

54   https://en.wikipedia.org/wiki/Abu_Bakr_al-Baghdadi

looking directly at the city of Duhok.[55] Duhok is a fairly large city nestled in a valley surrounded by mountains. A huge seal of Kurdistan made of painted rocks was on the mountainside overlooking the city.

As we drove through downtown, I was surprised how busy it was. It was clearly rush hour. Both the streets and sidewalks were full of pedestrians and traffic. The feeling of hope and change were in the air. It seemed that the city decided not to put life on hold despite the fact ISIS was 30 miles away. Similar to Israel, even though times were tough, the dream of a people having their own nation after thousands of years was a powerful force for excitement. For it was literally coming true before our eyes. We were witnessing the birth of a nation!

From the top floor of the hotel, Chuck pointed out a new soccer field that had not been used yet. The traffic was heavy. Chuck explained we were going to the church to prepare many bags containing two weeks of groceries for each family of four to distribute later.

After an hour of packing groceries, Daniel found a new soccer ball that had not been used yet. He left the work in the church courtyard and started kicking the ball in the empty residential street. It was a magnet. Local Muslim kids started appearing, leaving the safety of the gated home courtyard. Very quickly, Daniel found himself surrounded by dozens of laughing children trying to outmaneuver one another.

---

55 https://en.wikipedia.org/wiki/Dohuk

I wasn't the only parent watching the kids. Many of the kids' mothers wearing hijabs were watching from their second story balconies of their homes. I waved at one who also waved back. For a moment, everyone appeared to forget about the war and participated in what used to be a normal neighborhood activity.

As I watched Daniel and the local kids play soccer, I couldn't stop myself from smiling. Here we were, thousands of miles from home, in a neighborhood where the residents were scared to come outside. Yet, I could see the joy and innocence of each child. Even though the terror of ISIS had cast a long shadow over the entire region, God was going to use our team for something great.

Back at the hotel, Chuck reviewed the evening schedule for the team as we ate dinner. It was Sunday, and both churches expected us to participate in their services. Chuck explained that many church members had recently fled the city. There was also a prayer meeting scheduled in a home of a local Christian family. Chuck divided the nineteen of us into three teams to cover all three events. My team would go to the Methodist church Sunday night service. Another team would go to the WMA church service. The third team would go to the home prayer group meeting.

Since ISIS invaded Iraq, Duhok had taken in more than 70,000 refuges. Some of the homeless were now living in the churches. Team members were of varied backgrounds, cities, cultures, races, and denominations. Even though we were just getting to know each other, there was a palpable excitement that everyone shared. God had called us together to work for the glory of His Kingdom. As brothers and sisters in Christ, we were united to accomplish the mission that was ahead of us.

DISCUSSION QUESTIONS

- Do people worship Satan in modern times? In what nations?
- What instruction does the Bible give in dealing with this issue?

KEY TO SUCCESS

- When the Lord speaks to you, Listen. Even if you don't understand. All will be revealed in His time.

Sometimes Faith requires that you jump in with both feet without knowing the temperature of the water. Trust in the Lord and He will give you the tools you'll need to be successful in your calling.

The woman front and center in the white coat came to the church service as a distressed Yezidi refugee. She was dramatically delivered from demons and accepted Jesus Christ.

She left the church free and full of joy!

CHAPTER EIGHT

DEMON POSSESSED

"And these signs will accompany those who believe: In My name they will drive out demons; they will speak in new tongues; they will pick up snakes with their hands; and when they drink deadly poison, it will not hurt them at all; they will place their hands on sick people, and they will get well."   *Mark 16:17-18 NIV*

M y team consisted of three nurses and an elderly couple from Oregon, Len and Marie. Marie said she came on the trip because if something happened to Len, she did not want to be left behind, alone. We drove to the Methodist church in an urban neighborhood of homes side by side with small courtyards in front of each home. It was getting dark. I noticed the surrounding homes did not have their lights on.

Before the service began, the pastor told me, "Be careful what you do. If a Muslim becomes a Christian, they are going to get killed. We can't give Bibles to anyone if they did not ask for one because the government will shut us down." The first part of the service was in Arabic without a translator, so we politely tried to follow what was happening. A man came to the podium and passionately read a Bible passage. The three-man worship team used a keyboard and electric guitar and led worship songs I had not heard before. A church elder gave a short sermon. A translator came to the front, and our team was invited to speak.

After all three of our nurses had shared, it was finally my turn. I remembered the Lord's prophecy presented to me through Tim Storey about this trip. I told them that God loved them and that He wants to help them. I told them that God had told me that He had sent angels with our team to minister miracles and healing. If anyone wanted help, this was their moment to come forward, and we would ask God to help them.

Almost immediately, a young Yazidi woman stepped forward for prayer. Once I heard she was Yazidi, I knew she had been living her life under Satan's bondage. I also remembered the story I saw on CNN about the Yazidis who had been trapped on Sinjar Mountain attempting to flee ISIS fighters intent on killing them. After a few more questions, I found out that this woman was on that mountain during the news coverage and had survived almost certain death. She and her loved ones traveled 70 miles across the desert with only the clothes on their back to get to Duhok. She had lost many loved ones and neighbors along the journey, all of them murdered by ISIS. She and her relatives were currently living in an abandoned school near the church.

The translator explained that even before ISIS was an issue, she had a condition that had worsened over the last six years. Without warning, she would fall over, unconscious. She did not want to do that anymore. She closed her eyes and bowed her head when we said we would pray for her. As soon as I touched her forehead with oil on my fingers, she fell to the ground stiff like she was petrified. The posture she landed in was the posture she remained frozen in. As I knelt to help her, "You unclean spirits must leave in Jesus name!" shot out of my mouth spontaneously. She was unconscious, and respirations were not visible.

We lifted her into the front row of folding chairs and placed her on her side so her tongue would not fall back and obstruct her airway. I knelt by her face and could not see or hear evidence of her breathing. I held the back of my hand under her nose. I felt respirations. The nurses were simultaneously checking her neck and wrists for a pulse. The woman's arms and legs remained frozen in the position she landed in. Her head was also cocked to the side and now was held up in the air by her rigid neck. Several local women unsuccessfully tried to press her head down onto folded jackets so her neck would be supported. Other women tried to pry her teeth apart to force wadded paper in the side of her mouth as others dripped water from their fingertips onto her face. No effect. I motioned them away. Her head and limbs would not change position. I immediately knew it was not a seizure; it was not a hypoglycemic episode or any kind of medical condition. It was something I had read about in Matthew, Mark, Luke, John, and Acts and had never seen before in the United

States. It was a manifestation of a demonic possession.

I told everyone to pray, no spectators. The Worship team came to the front with their instruments and worshiped loudly. Len knelt beside me and placed his hand on her head and began to pray in tongues. As he did, his arm shook violently, but her head and neck remained fixed, extended in air immovable. The room was booming with prayers in different languages and unknown tongues. Each person had their hands stretched out, all calling on the Lord to help the woman. It was intense and loud! It must have looked chaotic to the unbelievers. It might have sounded like the original Pentecost. This was new spiritual territory for me. It also had to end well. The nurses and I kept praying while we repeatedly monitored her airway, respirations, and pulse. I had arrived with two large duffels and a suitcase of medicine, but medicine did not have the answer for this problem. Jesus was our only hope.

EXPERT WITNESSES

As we continued to pray for the young lady, her physical state did not improve. The more time that passed, the more concerned I became. After eight long minutes, I asked the church deacon if he had ever seen anything like this. "Once, but it didn't last this long." He replied. Tense expression was on every face.

Every medical team member was a seasoned healthcare provider from different fields of medicine. I was currently the Medical Director of a private hospital that served a city with a population of 100,000. I was also the ER physician for over 100 hours a week. Erroll Koshman was an ICU nurse in his 60s from British Columbia who cared for many cardiac patients. Julie Allen, RN, was an experienced hospice nurse from Arkansas in her 50s. Dawn Buschow, RN, was an experienced hospital nurse from Minnesota in her 50s. Each of us had expertise in varied fields of medical care. All of us were certain that we were dealing with a manifestation of demonic possession and not a medical or psychiatric condition. God had assembled a dream team of credible expert witnesses.

An epic struggle was occurring. The woman remained in catatonic rigidity with head held in the air. Despite forty minutes of Len's hand shaking violently, her head remained unmoved off the chair. Her eyes remained closed, and her face gave no grimace or expression. The loud prayers and electric instruments and singing were at an uncomfortable volume.

After forty minutes of praying, one of the Kurdish ladies who was a believer in Christ reached down and took a black cord off the girl's neck. She said in English, "God told me to do that." The girl started thrashing in the seats. The local women tried to restrain her arms without success. She had unusual strength as described with the man that had a legion of demons that Jesus rescued. She then grabbed her hair with both hands and started pulling. She was growling and grunting. The women were unable to remove her fingers from the hair. She tilted her head back, and a low howl came out of her mouth for what seemed like several minutes. Then she opened her eyes for the first time since she fell 45 minutes before. I had just seen something I had only read about before.

The room erupted in cheers. Dozens of locals yelled Hallelujahs and gave the Arabic La-la-la-la-las of victory. The worship and praise reverberated from the upper room church filling the dark and otherwise quiet neighborhood surrounding it.

Ladies sat the delivered woman up in the seat. She looked dazed. Her face was sweaty and pale. As people continued to celebrate, the woman who took the cord off the neck earlier knelt in front of the woman. She spoke in Arabic. The seated woman spoke back in a whisper. "Jesus." The Christian woman spoke again in Arabic. After a pause, the exhausted woman said "Jesus" louder. She appeared to catch her breath and said in a louder voice "Jesus," and a smile broke across her face for the first time that night. Shortly after, we led her to Christ.

A few minutes later, the woman who had just been delivered, appeared with a teenage girl and the translator. She explained that this was her little sister and she had the same problem. I said out loud, "I don't want to do that again." I was emotionally exhausted. Inspiration was given to me.

After putting my arm around the teenager's back to ensure she didn't fall and hit the tile floor like her older sister did, I said: "I'm going to tell you the best news in the world." Through our Chaldean Catholic translator, I told the teenage Yazidi girl the Good News of the Gospel and asked her if she wanted to pray and accept Jesus as her Lord and Savior. Smiling with big bright eyes and shaking her head she said yes. She repeated the prayer of the translator and accepted the Lord. Bracing myself, I touched her forehead with oil on my left hand, and she immediately went limp, completely unconscious as I supported her with my right arm. After just three minutes, she came to. As opposed to her sister's 45-minute ordeal, resultant headache and exhaustion, this teenager came to alert, strong and smiling! The gathering erupted in more praise and thanksgiving to God. Everyone was taking selfies; it was a tremendous celebration!

The elder gave our team a ride to our hotel from the church in his car. We were the only car I saw on the road at that late hour. I did not notice any home on the way with lights on. The elder said, "That was an unusual night at church." After a moment of reflection, he turned to me and said: "But maybe it should not be."

MORE THAN ENOUGH

On day two, I woke with a lot on my mind. Before I left for Iraq, I had expectations of what the trip would be like. The events of the night had changed everything. I had planned on providing medical care and sharing the Gospel. But God had extra plans. God was going to do much more than I had previously imagined. I was excited.

After breakfast, all nineteen of the mission team gathered to give reports of the day before and pray. All were amazed by each team's praise reports of miracles and salvations. The home prayer group had received a call from Syria while in prayer. A believer had called for prayer of a loved one with terminal colon cancer.

The patient was in the hospital actively bleeding, and the doctors said there was nothing else they could offer. The doctors estimated she would be dead in three hours. We prayed again for that and other needs.

As we began to set up our medical clinic in the church sanctuary, I was so impressed by how gracious the local Christians were toward our team. At first, they all looked the same to me. After working alongside them, I began to realize that the local congregation was as ethnically diverse as our mission team. A few Christians were Arab, others were Chaldean, and many were Kurds. They often spoke different languages. Yet, in the same way, God had brought our mission team together. They also had a beautiful spirit of unity, all for His greater purpose.

It was Paul who told the Ephesians, "Make every effort to maintain the unity of the Spirit in the bond of peace." That first day in Iraq, I began to better understand what Paul meant by that. There was a power that came from our unity as brothers and sisters in Christ. The closer we worked together, the more I was convinced God would do more great things through us.

NEW CHRISTIANS ARE LED BY THE SPIRIT

Another young lady, who was brought in by her mother, had the same problem of falling over unconscious. She did not want that anymore, so she came into the clinic and told the nurses that she had this issue. While she was there, she fell over just like the girl at the church service had done. The nurses knew what this was and had seen it end well before, so they started praying. The girl was down just a moment when the first girl that we had spent forty-five minutes with the night before came running through the open doorway and fell on the girl on the floor. Lying on the unconscious girl, she broke into wailing and crying and yelling one word over and over. She yelled Jesus!

The nurses did not know that they knew each other, so they tried to pull the girl off of the unconscious girl on the floor, but she would not leave. She unwound the black cord from the young girl's neck, and immediately the young girl started regaining consciousness. We found out that she was another little sister of our first convert. The mother that brought the young girl to the clinic told the translator, "I saw souls come out of my daughter," and proceeded to tell their story.

Six years before, her husband, the girls' father, was killed by an exploding bomb. The family was not doing well, so the mother brought the family to the Yazidi shaman. He did rituals, anointing each child with oils and put a black cord around their necks. In the following weeks, they noticed little change. However, slowly life got a little worse every month and year that followed. Each member of the family experienced worsening physical and mental health. The first convert who was just used by God had been in the worst condition. She had recently been diagnosed with schizophrenia by local Arab doctors who unsuccessfully tried to control her actions with high doses of anti-psychotic medications. The mother told us, "I brought my family to the Yazidi leaders and my family got worse and worse but then

I bring my children here, and they get better. I want to become a Christian." Both the mother and daughter became Christians.

There is power in the name of Jesus. When I look back in the Bible, there are stories about people who don't even like Jesus trying to use His name to cast out demons, Acts 19:13-17, for example. Everybody who went on the trip was there for the purpose to honor Jesus, and even though we were all from different denominations, we all had the same heart.

SPIRITUAL AMBUSH IN THE STREET

The Kurdish military is called the Peshmerga,[56] which translates into The Confronters of Death. They are the sworn enemies of ISIS. They are who you see on the news, fighting against all the odds, to defeat ISIS who have possessions of tanks and military equipment that the Iraqi soldiers left behind when they deserted. The Peshmerga have been fighting for a long time.

The church clinic became the talk of the town after several days. Most of the people we treated were not Christians; we were non-stop busy. It was a great honor to have a Peshmerga officer come with his family to receive care. The next day, he brought one of his soldiers for treatment as well. I invited them to return to the church at 7:00 p.m. that night to hear the Good News.

The officer and soldier came with their wives and children. The men and their sons sat with me along the back row on the left side of the room. Their wives and daughters sat on the other

---

56   https://en.wikipedia.org/wiki/Peshmerga

side. I noticed them as they watched the well-spirited teenagers hanging out in the side room and the men and women sitting together in front of them. Chuck quietly made his way to each mission team telling us to be thoughtful about our words because many Muslims had come to the service. I felt that God had directed me to pray a blessing on the Kurds and their dream of a nation of their own (Kurdistan). This was confirmed when Chuck whispered to me that I was to give the Benediction at the end of the service.

The officer flipped his cell open and showed me pictures of him with other soldiers in the war with artillery and large fixed machine guns overlooking the valley below. I showed them pictures from my cell as we waited for the service to begin.

I raised my hands during the worship and praised God and sang with my eyes closed. I opened them briefly to see the soldier next to me with his hands raised as well. The officer's cell rang as the music was ending. Both men repeatedly bowed as they quietly slipped out the door. Their families stayed for the rest of the service.

I led the fellowship in a prayer of blessing on the dream of Kurdistan becoming a nation for the Kurds. We prayed for protection for the Peshmerga soldiers and victory over ISIS. Snacks and drinks were prepared for celebration afterward. I saw the car pull in front of the church courtyard to drive us to the hotel. I went down the outside stairs across the church courtyard and closed the gate behind me. I felt strong, alert and energized all evening but that changed as I exited the church property. I walked around the car to the front passenger door and immediately was struck with convulsing rigors. I could not stay still. I was shaking, and my teeth were chattering. I felt weak and was having a hard time keeping my eyes open or holding my head up. I have never felt that way before. I asked James, a Baptist pastor on the mission team, who got in the seat behind me to pray for me. He could see what was happening and placed his hand on my back and started to pray. Pastor Armen, the local pastor, came outside to say good-bye and looked at me with concern. He placed his hand on my chest through the rolled down the window and prayed. I felt relief while he prayed but the symptoms returned when he stopped. We were dropped off at the hotel.

Julie, the hospice nurse, and her husband stopped by my room and asked through the open door if I wanted them to pray. While they were close to me with their hands on me, I felt less miserable. When they moved away, I felt worse. They left promising to continue to pray.

The rigors and weakness tormented me all night. Ibuprofen, Tylenol, and antibiotics had no effect. It was a night of prayer and suffering. While praying in the spirit, an understanding came to me. I understood through prayer that Yazidi wrongful prayers were enabling this attack. I also understood that the pictures taken of me the first night of celebrating at the Methodist church were somehow a factor. I had picked a fight with the spiritual forces behind ISIS by praying for the Peshmerga and the defeat of ISIS. I fell into a fitful sleep in the morning.

I woke to see I had missed breakfast. At 10:00 a.m., the symptoms stopped, and my strength increased every minute. I realized that the team was in prayer for me at the moment. I got myself showered and ready for the medical clinic. When I appeared in the lobby with the duffels of medicine everyone was surprised; several team members suggested I stay and rest. I felt much better and was NOT going to miss what the devil had tried to stop.

We loaded into the white mini-vans and headed out of town. We drove about 10 miles out of the city to a Yazidi refugee camp. Jesus said in Matthew 25:40, "Whatever you have done to the least of these you have done to Me." It was not even an official refugee camp—it did not have all the facilities, just had some tents. The refugees' desire was to have an outhouse with privacy for the women. They had lived there for months, only had some running water out of a well, a little bit of electricity and the free tents that were donated from the United Kingdom. It was one tent for a family, and each tent had a mattress.

We only visited this Yazidi refugee camp one time. World Missions Alliance had purchased blankets in advance to hand out, so that day we passed out blankets and food, as well as did a medical clinic. I saw all kinds of illnesses there. People are people, so I saw all the things that happen to everybody such as diabetes and high blood pressure. The folks that were there had run for their lives and had no medicine or no money to buy medicine if they had diabetes or high blood pressure. Chronic health conditions were way out of control. Fortunately, we had lots of medicines, so we were able to get many patients' symptoms back under control, so they did not have a stroke or heart attack. This camp had a huge outbreak of pneumonia and bronchitis—a lot of sick people with respiratory problems. We were able to start them on antibiotics and turn that around before it became life threatening.

While we were there, a mother brought her five-year-old son. She told the nurses that his eyes rolled back and he had fallen unconscious; she wanted to help her son. At this point, without me even being part of this conversation, the nurses said, "Does he have a thing around his neck?"

She said, "Yes, that's our magic."

They said, "You'll have to take that off for him to get better."

She said, "No, that's our magic. I'm not going to take that off." I never saw the boy, she just left.

Mostly, though, the kids were normal kids, just victims of the system they had been raised in. I saw a lot of vitamin deficiencies, things we do not normally see here in the States. You can imagine that after several months of starving and stress, kids had hair falling out, rashes and illnesses or conditions that are commonly known to be vitamin deficiencies. Again, I was thankful for my friend, Danny, who had loaded me up with a lot of vitamins. We were able to turn that around for a lot of these children.

Another thing we helped with at the refugee camp was to distribute food. The mission team gave a bag of groceries to each tent.

We left the camp on a beautiful autumn evening. The next

day, a cold front hit Kurdistan with freezing wind gusts. Many of the folks we helped by giving them blankets and medicine would have died from exposure and pneumonia without that timely intervention! The Lord is sovereign, and His timing is perfect!

One night, we had a church service with many Muslims in attendance. Fifteen came in with the Muslim religion and went out as born again Christians. They heard the Good News for the first time and believed. They thought they were going to die because that was the threat of murder for converting from Muslim to Christian. Even so, they were willing to come forward during the service and pray out loud publicly accepting Jesus Christ as Lord. They later walked out of the church to face their fate. As Revelation 12:11 says, "They triumphed over him (Satan) by the blood of the Lamb and by the word of their testimony; they did not love their lives so much as to shrink from death."

They did not get killed. The threat was an empty threat. The enemy can't follow through on ALL his threats. Thirty miles away, there were people being crucified and ISIS was cutting off the heads of children and women. Muslims killing Muslims sometimes, but they are horrific against the born again Christians as well. These people that came to church that night were brave enough to accept the Good News and be public about it.

DISCUSSION QUESTIONS

- I have wondered many times after what would have happened if we did not continue to pray for 45 minutes.

How many times have I stopped praying because I got distracted or fatigued or lazy? Could this be one reason why we don't always have results?

- How much training does a Christian need before they can be used by God?

- What does the Bible teach about demons?

- Has God asked you to "Go unto all the nations"?

- Have you ever had to suffer because of your faith in Christ?

KEY TO SUCCESS

- Pray the specific need until you are released by the Holy Spirit. The burden to pray for that need will be lifted.

- Pray out loud.

- The more Christians praying in agreement the better.

- Fasting augments prayer.

- Anointing with oil is honoring the Scripture in James and God rewards your obedience.

- Praying God's Word is powerful. Praying in the Spirit allows the Holy Spirit to pray a perfect prayer out of your mouth.

The last day of our mission trip Kurdish soldiers disclosed to us that our team had been protected by undercover soldiers during our entire trip in Kurdistan.

Miracles In Our Midst

Mark 16:16-18 & James 5:13-16 – Many Iraqi people were instantly healed during prayer.

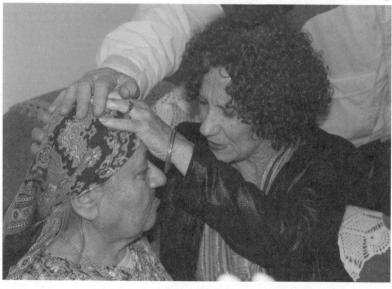

CHAPTER NINE

REVENGE OR FORGIVENESS

"The weapons we fight with are not the weapons of the world. On the contrary, they have divine power to demolish strongholds."
2 Corinthians 10:4 NIV

At our medical clinic in the city, the triage area was set up for the nurses to see our patients in the sanctuary first. The patients would then be treated by me in the pastor's office in private. After a few days, word about the clinic had spread all over the city. By now we were treating more Muslims and Yazidis than Christians. A friendly rapport started to become established between the Muslims and the Christians. During our time there, we heard several stories of people spending all the money they had to buy a taxi ride from the other side of the city to come to our clinic. It didn't matter that we were Christian and they were Muslim. They knew they had diabetes or high blood pressure and needed help and didn't have enough money to come back a second time. We invited many to come back to our nightly church service. After a few nights, we had more Muslims in the church services than Christians. In the clinic, we told people we treated that we were there in the name of Jesus because He told us to help them. A lot of respect was given to the Christians by Muslims and vice versa.

Something I noticed when I spoke to patients was whenever I said the word "forgive" or "forgiveness," even if it was off handed, if they were Muslim, it offended them, and they got angry. It was simply not a part of their mindset. It is not an idea taught in the Koran or something they believe. The Muslims wanted to get even with whoever wronged them; they would start ranting on how they wanted justice and how they wanted the terrorists to pay. I also saw Christians who had suffered the same or more, and they were willing to forgive. It became evident when put side by side, that Christianity was different. It involved forgiveness.

We believe that when we are forgiven, we are supposed to forgive others. That is a core idea within Christianity that is unique to itself. There is a movement being talked about right now called Chrislam where people say we all worship the same God and we all are working together, but it is a lie. I have seen Christianity and Islam side by side. It is not the same.

A KNIFE IN CHURCH

Erroll told me about some excitement that nurses in the church sanctuary experienced during triage. A newly-wed Yazidi couple came to the clinic for help. The bride had a condition that caused her to collapse unconscious without warning. The nurse asked if she had a black cord around her neck. The bride collapsed in the church. The nurse told the groom that the cord needed to be removed for her to get better. The young man produces a wicked looking hunting knife causing several people to gasp. He brings the knife to her throat and cuts the cord from her neck. The bride recovers and the nurses lead the couple to the Lord.

GRAND FINALE

The last day of clinic started with a bang! Remember the woman that had been bleeding to death in a Syrian hospital from terminal cancer with only 3 hours left to live? She was our first patient! She said the bleeding stopped and she walked out of the hospital after the prayer over the phone. Then she traveled out of the Syrian Civil War across the ISIS controlled territory of Iraq to come to our church clinic to tell us Jesus had healed her.

Different from past clinics, we saw many cancer patients. A 30-year-old Muslim man had kidney cancer. He could not afford care after he was diagnosed by local doctors and came to our clinic for help. Our faith was increased for Jesus to heal people from cancer. I presented the Good News. He was eager to pray and ask Jesus to save and heal him.

An older Christian lady who had a mastectomy and chemo for end-stage breast cancer came for help. We anointed and prayed for her. After prayer, she told us that Jesus told her, "Whatever they ask for, I will do."

The nurse peeked in the pastor's office where I examined patients. She told me there was a lady who she did not think I would be able to help. I know I can't help but Jesus can. The lady was very depressed because her daughter was murdered.

The woman told us that when ISIS came to Mosul, most of the residents expected the Iraqi army to defeat ISIS quickly. The woman lived with her daughter, and they chose to hide at home until ISIS was dealt with. After leaving the house to get groceries for only 30 minutes, she found her daughter on fire in front of her home. Her daughter had been raped by the terrorists and then set on fire while she was still alive. Neighbors helped her take her daughter to a local hospital, but the daughter died. She had pictures of her burnt daughter in an envelope that she always carried. It was all she had to remember her by. The nurse brought her back to the room I used to examine people. The elder of the church told her, "You can't keep crying. You're crying every day, and you need to move on." I asked if we could pray for her.

We anointed the lady, while still keeping our hands on her we closed our eyes. I told her that while we prayed, I felt that the Lord wanted her to give those pictures to the pastor so he could deal with them respectfully, and she did. Then Sheila, another lady that was on our team told her, "We're going to pray that Jesus will give you happy pictures to remember your daughter in place of the pictures you are willing to give up in obedience." As we prayed together, I felt the woman changing.

The lady started laughing and said that she could see her daughter in Jesus' arms, smiling. She took one picture out of the envelope, the only happy picture to remember her daughter by. She forgave the unforgivable. In contrast, I saw Muslims who were unable to forgive their car being stolen or their house being stolen, and their lives being turned upside down. I continue to stand amazed at what a Christian can do with God's help—forgive the unforgivable.

GOD'S PROTECTION

On the last day of the trip, while we were in the medical clinic, another part of the team was up on a mountain between the cities of Duhok and Mosul. Mosul is controlled by ISIS. Our team went up on the mountain where they could overlook both Duhok and Mosul. A lady on our team brought a guitar to lead worship songs and pray. Daniel, my son, was up there with them.

A little farther up the mountain from where the mission group gathered was a lone sentry. Under the Kurdistan flag on a thin pole sat a Peshmerga soldier on a folding chair with a machine gun and a radio. He was stationed to look toward Mosul, ISIS headquarters, to see if they were coming to attack Duhok.

The soldier heard the music, and it prompted him to come closer. Our team asked if they could take a picture with him. He said no, that he would have to talk to his commander about it. He came back twenty minutes later with his commander. Our team found out that the soldier was originally from Mosul. Even though he was now a Peshmerga soldier and a sworn enemy of ISIS, he still had loved ones in Mosul. He did not want his picture on the internet. His loved ones might then be killed by ISIS in retaliation. He ended up taking pictures with our team wearing a ski-mask so his features would stay indistinguishable.

When the commander came closer to the group, our team started to tell them who they were. He interrupted and said, "I know who you are, I know what you've been doing. We've been watching over you for ten days! I knew you were coming up here before you got here. I got a radio call that you were coming. Those people that work in the hotel where you are staying—they don't work there. They are undercover police and undercover soldiers to protect you. The whole ten days we have been there to protect you."

The soldier from Mosul had pulled a velcro military patch off his shoulder and gave it to the lady worship leader. He hoped that the patch would remind our team to pray for his family. The lady with the guitar gave a silk scarf to the young soldier as a gift.

Now, we understood that many of the Peshmerga soldiers were not Christian, but they secretly protected our team while we went from church to church during the trip as we shared the Gospel. They protected us while Muslims, sometimes fifteen at a time, accepted Jesus Christ as Lord. They saw all kinds of miracles. They heard reports of the people that were demon possessed being delivered. When we left, we had great respect for the Peshmerga and Kurdish people.

The Peshmerga soldiers protected us the entire time while we were not aware of their presence. I was aware that we had heavenly warriors also watching over us as well. I am reminded of Hebrews 12:1 and continue to walk with confidence knowing that, "Therefore, since we are surrounded by so great a cloud of witnesses, let us also lay aside every weight, and sin which clings so closely, and let us run with endurance the race that is set before us."

AMBUSH AND CHECKPOINTS

Daniel and I had to leave that last evening, earlier than the rest of the mission team to catch our flight out of Iraq. The rest of the team left us at the hotel and departed in the two minivans to go to dinner. Fifteen minutes later, the young lady who had led the worship with her guitar on the mountain that day comes back ill. She was suddenly struck with a profound weakness and shaking chills without fever or other symptoms. Daniel and I anoint and pray for her. She says she feels better while we pray but worse when we stop. I say I understood because the same thing happened to me. I heard later that next morning she recovered immediately as the team prayed for her.

A young man arrived in a car to drive us from our hotel in

Duhok back across the desert to the Erbil airport. We drove on a moonless night across the desert. The drive was tense. We listened to his CD of Christian music in Arabic as we headed toward Mosul. I had spoken to my son, Ben, back home that evening and learned that the U.S. had bombed an ISIS target in Mosul the night before. The driver turned the car radio off as we approached wary soldiers at a checkpoint. After a brief exchange between one of the soldiers and the driver, I slowly retrieved my passport and passed it to the soldier. He disappeared into a small guard stand for a few minutes only to reappear, return my passport and wave us through. No traffic tonight. I softly prayed in tongues to the music. We could see the glow of Mosul lights in the sky. We had to make sure we did NOT miss our turn toward Erbil and end up in ISIS-controlled Mosul. The U.S. bombing put Abu Bakr al-Baghdadi in a Mosul hospital and killed his number one lieutenant. The driver spoke little English. He would tell me the name of each abandoned village we drove through. I would try to repeat the name but kept failing. Eventually, he would give up on correcting me, and we would laugh. The laughter lightened up the atmosphere.

We could see a lone soldier standing by a barrel containing a fire setting the sky aglow in the middle of the road. It was bitterly cold tonight under the cloudless sky. He took my passport and smiling spoke to the driver while nodding and looking me in the eye. The driver said, "He wants to know if you enjoyed your stay in Kurdistan." I said, "I love Kurdistan and the Kurdish people." After the driver explained to the soldier, he smiled and nodded repeatedly to me. As we drove away, he looked so exposed standing by himself in the light of the fire surrounded by the dark open desert. What a desperate situation he was in. And he was concerned about me having a pleasant stay like a cruise ship captain asking a departing guest if they were pleased? Wow.

BEST NEWS IN THE WORLD

Good News! The good news of the Gospel doesn't hurt anybody. I am a doctor and often share the Good News with patients in my office. I'll tell them, "I want to tell you the best news in the world." You can do the same. We know stuff that a lot of others don't know. That's why we are here. Our job is to tell the Good News—and it is good news. You won't hurt anybody—I've already tested it, and haven't hurt anybody. You can't mess it up—it's good news. You tell what you believe.

I have my way of presenting the Gospel. I usually tell them it's the best news in the world. Nobody is perfect, everyone makes mistakes. God knew everyone would make mistakes because he knows everything. Out of love, He sent His only son, Jesus, to pay the price on the cross so you can have the free gift of life. It's like someone trying to give you a birthday present; it's not yours until you accept it. I'll ask, "Have you heard that before?"

A lot of times they will say, "No, I've not heard that." They may have a cross on their neck. Some will have tattoos of crosses. Sometimes, a person will tell me they have Bibles at home.

Sometimes, a person will tell me they have been going to church for twenty years, but they are "not ready yet." You can be the one, just like Phillip talking to that Ethiopian eunuch in Acts 8. You can be there at that moment for a baby to be born into the Kingdom of God and for their new life to start. They have to start sometime—that doesn't mean that is the whole story, but the story of a new life has to be started.

We have the privilege right now to tell people the Good News so they can accept Christ. Choosing to be witnesses of His Good News is "to live is Christ and to die is gain". Right now, our job is to promote Jesus. Where we are is where we are supposed to be sharing the Good News, whether it is in my office or in a parking lot when a homeless person asks for money. When you have a captive audience, it could be a divine appointment. I've had that happen when a homeless person cornered me in a restaurant parking lot. It's just a matter of looking for the Divine appointments. Lord, open our eyes so we see those opportunities. Many Divine appointments I've missed but let's go forward and not miss any more than we have to.

CONCLUSION

Jesus is Faithful! I saw Him answer prayer in desperate circumstances. I saw Him deliver young people from generational bondage and demon-possession. I saw people who were healed from terminal illness by Jesus. I saw God's favor fall on local believers as they served their neighbors. I gained more perspective, new faith, and big expectations for what the Lord can do with people who surrender to His Great Commission to make disciples of all nations (Matthew 28:19). I got to see how people gave unselfishly to see the Bible published in a new language. I saw a friend give medicine and supplies so that we could successfully run a clinic and provide what the Kurds needed for their health. I saw people from different nations and languages work together to bring hope to the patients we worked for in The Name of Jesus. I am so thankful I could bring my son to experience the presence and move of God together as history-making events were unfolding before the whole world.

DISCUSSION QUESTIONS

- Have you ever noticed seasons or days where the focus was specific?
- How do Christianity, Islam and Yazidi faiths differ? What do they have in common?
- What does the Bible say about the Medes?
- What prophecy in the Bible speaks about the future of the Assyrians? (Mosul)
- What words do you use to share the Best News in the World?

KEY TO SUCCESS

- Forgive everyone of everything, even if you don't feel like it.

Know your enemy. The anti-Christ spirit denies that Jesus is the only begotten Son of God who has been raised from the dead and is alive. Christ is the only one who can save men's souls and give eternal life.

Chuck Todd, President of World Missions Alliance & Pastor Armen distribute food and blankets to Yezidi refugees.

CHAPTER TEN

ON EARTH
AS IN HEAVEN

"They will neither harm nor destroy on all my holy mountain, for the earth will be filled with the knowledge of the Lord as the waters cover the sea."   *Isaiah 11:9 NIV*

Since my 2014 trip to Kurdistan, a great many things have transpired, all of which continue to bear witness to the goodness and glory of God. World Missions Alliance laid a foundation to serve in the Middle East. Odd Frustol and others set up a six-month **pastors training** program in the Republic of Georgia for Kurdish Christians. Many Kurds living in Georgia, who have felt the call of God to become full-time ministers, have completed that training and now serve as ministers among the Kurds in the war-torn countries of Syria, Iraq, and Georgia.

Due to the success of the Kurdish military's campaign against

ISIS over the past two years, many towns and territory that were once under ISIS's control have now been reclaimed. This has meant that many of the refugee camps our team visited while in Kurdistan are now vacant, with many returning home. World Missions Alliance has received many reports of Kurds, who after coming to Christ through our efforts, have now returned home, eagerly sharing the good news of the Gospel with their friends and family.

The initial bonds between Chuck Todd and the new Kurdistan government that was the origin or our opportunity have only grown stronger in the last two years. In November 2016, Chuck Todd and the World Missions Alliance team were escorted by a high-ranking Peshmerga general through the towns and churches that were recovered from ISIS just days and weeks before.

The gifts of food and toiletries that were given through World Missions Alliance to the families of Kurdish soldiers, all in the name of Jesus, led to the production of a television special about the positive message of Christianity that aired on the national Kurdish Television network.

The Methodist Church my team and I visited in Duhok has grown from a weekly attendance of 20 to over 80 within the last two years. They are currently in the process of adding a third story to their church facility. The Word Missions Alliance non-denomination church is also growing in attendance. Both congregations have been blessed with great favor by the government and local neighbors.

Since the days of my journey in Kurdistan, my life has been

immeasurably blessed. I don't go on missions because I'm an American or a Texan; because I'm Protestant or Charismatic; or not because I'm Caucasian. There are faults with every earthly culture, label, or body politic we often identify ourselves with that run contrary to what God wants to do. Each of these things is not enough reason in themselves to leave my family and responsibilities that God has entrusted to me back home. Rather, it is because Jesus said to go, so I go.

I have confidence that I am doing His will. That when I'm away and unavailable on the mission field, He covers me by taking care of the things back home (family well-being, career, finances, etc.). For the God of the Bible is a God who is our protector.

Romans 8:28 says, *"He makes all things work together for good for those who love God and are called according to His purposes."*

Richard Bartlett, MD

AUTHOR BIO

Richard Bartlett, MD is the recipient of the Meritorious Service Award from the Texas Health and Human Services Commission. The governor of Texas appointed him to the newly created Texas Health Disparities Task Force in February 2002. It was a two-year assignment to advise the Governor, Lt. Governor, and Speaker of the House on how to improve access to quality healthcare for all Texans. He was reappointed year after year for seven years.

In support of the U.S. war heroes, he was the first physician to travel on the Inaugural Honor Flights of the Permian Basin and South Plains of Texas.

Dr. Bartlett has served as Medical Director of multiple public and private ambulance services, clinics, hospitals, nursing homes, and emergency rooms. He has served four terms as President of a county Medical Society. He has been the CBS News Medical Expert of West Texas for 20 years.

Dr. Bartlett served four terms as County Medical Society President and as Vice President of the local Head Start program. He continues to practice medicine and lives in West Texas with his wife and seven children.